# Enlightened Minds

# Enlightened Minds

Dr. A.P.J. Abdul Kalam

*Edited by*

Arun Tiwari

*Published by*
**PRABHAT PRAKASHAN PVT. LTD.**
4/19 Asaf Ali Road,
New Delhi-110 002 (INDIA)
e-mail: prabhatbooks@gmail.com

ISBN 978-93-86300-15-7
**ENLIGHTENED MINDS**
*by* Dr. A.P.J. Abdul Kalam



*Edition*
2025

*Price*
₹ 400.00 (Rupees Four Hundred only)

*Printed at*
Narula Printers, Delhi

*I place this book at the feet of Shri A.P.J.M. Maracayer, Dr. Kalam's elder brother on the occasion of his completing 100 years in this world, in anticipation that the soul body of Dr. Kalam will be pleased with my effort.*

**—Arun Tiwari**

# Editorial

Dr. A.P.J. Abdul Kalam had an incredible passion for enlightening the youth and he made this process of interacting with young students, his lifetime mission, after surviving a helicopter crash landing at Ranchi. There were many questions that came to his mind, like: Do the youth really know the meaning of development in India? What type of understanding do the youth have towards development? Are they really concerned about the development and the future of India? To address these questions and to understand the mind frame of children, he started with a resolution of meeting a million children which eventually turned out to be a historical achievement of meeting 150 million children, during his lifetime. His final moments, on the 27 of July 2016, was spent in front of the students of the Indian Institute of Management (IIM) Shillong. I have accompanied Dr. Kalam to hundreds of such interactions and have always marvelled at the ease with which he inspired the youth to give value and self-love to themselves and to take responsibility for their lives through the discovery of their passions.

Post the book, *Wings of Fire* written in the year 1999, I have had the privilege of seeing thousands of young people, writing to Dr. Kalam, about how they started to follow their passion and began to live the life of their dreams. It is a fact that through his books and speeches, Dr. Kalam has worked with the youth to uncover and discover their passions, which has eventually helped them in living a life filled with joy and success. A large number of Indian youth, today, are capable, devoted, dedicated idealists and hardworking.

There is no doubt that there is a lot of strength, power and capability in the youth of today.

The collection of some of Dr. Kalam's speeches, presented in this book, are indeed a methodically developed tool, which educates people on how to discover their passions and uncover their potential. A greater involvement of youth, not just in their homes, but also in their schools and community will benefit not only their socio-economic environment but also help in capacity and personal development.

Though Dr. Kalam focussed on kids and teens, individually, as well as in social settings, he also worked with adults. He guided everyone on how best to recognize and break limiting beliefs and pointed them in the direction of the next best step to be taken to achieve success in life. Dr. Kalam encouraged everyone to live their life on Wings. Therefore, through this book, you can identify the areas in your life wherein you can achieve major success. Through the 25 speeches of Dr. Kalam, this book is a good teacher on various aspects such as, how to build ideal relationships that are key to a fulfilling life, how to create balance in various aspects of life, and how to live satisfying, successful and passionate lives.

My heartfelt thanks to Dr. A.P.J.M. Nazema Maraikayar, Dr. Kalam's niece and his literary heiress, who authorized the publication of these speeches. I also thank Prabhat Prakashan, who has been publishing books for and on Dr. Kalam right from the first book *"India 2020"* which was published in the year 1996 and who has now helped in bringing out this book as well. I can say this with certainty that this book will surely help readers in experiencing the joy of living a passionate and a purposeful life and to stop dwelling on setbacks and lacks, and take action to create that purposeful life and begin to experience the life lived by the top 5% of the population around the world.

**—Arun Tiwari**

Hyderabad
November 2016

# 1
# Innovation Amongst Youth

## Innovation is the Capital

I was studying the Global Competitiveness Report. There I find in terms of Innovative Capacity Index US is ranked one, Singapore 6, South Africa 27, China 40, Brazil 42 and India 44. In the same report I noticed that the proportion of Scientists and Engineers Index is stated as US 4, Singapore 6, South Africa 38, China 43, Brazil 51 and India 60. Thus, we can see the large proportion of new ideas and innovation are generated in the Universities in USA. This innovation arises from private sector initiative and the R & D productivity of the firm, shaped by local policies and nature of local institutions. National innovative capacity has to be the country's important potential to reinforce both political and economic entity with commercially relevant competitive products. This capacity is distinct from purely scientific or technical achievements and focuses on the economic application of new technology. Thus, for building innovative capacity, we require the partnership of private sector, public sector, R&D and academia as a group recommend the universities is work towards building the innovative capacity amongst its faculty and impart knowledge with students.

To achieve a goal what is needed is not only knowledge, but also a passion. The passion should not be limited to the technical aspects but it should also aim towards creating a concern for the society with a view to finding positive solutions to the problems.

## Team Building

In the present day world when the corpus of known knowledge is multidisciplinary and products and services are complex, it is often not possible to have a loner as an innovator. Most of the discoveries and innovation are team efforts. Education system should work towards team building among the students. Every student must have an opportunity to play the role of a team member and a team leader so that he can see both sides of the fence. The amount of information that we have around us is overwhelming. The management of knowledge therefore must move out of the realm of the individual and shift into the realm of the networked groups. The students must learn how to manage knowledge collectively. When the information is networked the power and utility of the information grows as squared as predicted by Metcalfe's law. Information that is static does not grow. In the new digital economy, information that is circulated creates innovation and contributes to national wealth. In this context, let us discuss the national scenario and its priorities.

## Young Innovators

The creativity is indeed the result of the education process and the environment of the school and above all the teachers' capability in igniting the minds of the students. The essence of it can be seen in the following verses:

- Learning gives creativity.
- Creativity leads to thinking.
- Thinking provides knowledge.
- Knowledge makes you great.

## Creativity

Since our population is of a billion people, the society

in its own way has to make innovations continuously, not only in urban areas but also in rural areas. For example, the honey bee network movement is an excellent attempt. Creativity comes from beautiful minds. It can be anywhere and any part of the country. It may start from a fisherman hamlet or a farmer's household or a dairy farm or cattle breeding centre or it emanates from class rooms or labs or industries or R&D centres. Creativity has got multi-dimensions like inventions, discoveries and innovations. Creativity has got an ability to imagine or invent something new by combining, changing or reapplying existing ideas. Creativity has an attitude to accept change and newness, a willingness to play with ideas and possibilities, a flexibility of outlook, the habit of enjoying the good, while looking for ways to improve it. Creativity has a process to work hard and continually to improve ideas and solutions by making gradual alterations and refinements to their works. The important aspect of creativity is: seeing the same thing as everybody else, but thinking of something different.

## Innovation

Innovation is market-driven. Innovation can also be making improved performance of the product/system technique by adopting a change using most alternative technologies. An innovative product makes a leap in the benefits-to-costs ratio in some area of endeavour. Innovation is a systematic, organised, rational work usually done in many stages like analysis, tests, experiment etc. I would like to give a few examples of innovative technologies/applications. What we see in optical communications is speed vs cost. In flexible manufacturing systems it is choice vs cost. In the web-enabled processes, it is customer satisfaction vs cost. Again in e-Mail, a message is instantly delivered in any part of the world through internet.

**Building Innovation System**

It is through the process of innovation that knowledge is converted into wealth and social good. Further, innovation is an important factor for the competitiveness of both service and manufacturing sectors. Innovation tends to emanate less from R&D and more from other sources, including organizational change. Hence there is an urgent need to establish an efficient innovation system in the country. Such a system would involve creation of clusters, which are networks of interdependent firms, knowledge producing institutions (universities, colleges/institutes, research institutes, technology providing firms), bridging institutions (e.g. think tanks, providers of technical or consultancy services), and customers linked in a value-addition creating production chain. The concept of clusters goes beyond that of a firm network, as it captures all forms of knowledge sharing and exchange. Thus, an innovative system with its clusters would tap into the growing stock of global knowledge, assimilate and adapt it to local needs and finally create new knowledge and technology.

**Partnership**

The National Innovation Foundation is able to attract number of innovations coming from the rural sector. However, what they need is design input to make it into a competitive marketable product. I would recommend a collaborative venture between the National Institute of Design and National Innovation Foundation to work on converting the promising innovations into a commercially viable venture. This can lead to creation of a number of enterprises in the rural sector leading to large-scale employment opportunity and wealth generation in the rural areas. The establishment of enterprises for such ventures can be financially supported by the Technology Development Board which is part of the Department of Science and Technology.

**Conclusion**

Innovation at the rural area: Search and locate any ambient innovations competencies, recognize promising innovations and assist through Self Help Groups. As a next stage systematic design of the innovation can be supported by institutions like NID transforming it into a business proposition. At this stage banks should provide venture capital. Once the production stabilizes in small-scale, it can be extended to large commercial production through the assistance of Technology Development Board. These enterprises should preferably be located in the rural sector where the raw material and the inputs will be available. Also there is a need to train the local youth for undertaking the production and marketing operation.

□

*Addressing the Presentation of 3rd Annual Award Distribution Function of National Innovation Foundation, Ahmedabad on 05-01-2005.*

# 2
# Beautiful Minds

A German Girl Anthea Neums brought out her imagination of how the season of Easter looks like in the rural environment; the bright colours that she has chosen reminded me of my home town on the seashore, where I spent my childhood days. In the same book, 14 year girl Supraja Chakravarthy, from India narrates a story about the homely middle class morality and how the votes are purchased during an election. It is clear that the young mind wants a change.

Aardhra Krishna (13), has worn her thinking cap on and let her imagination fly. She has visualised how the earth will look like around 3000 AD. In her imagination, the citizens are forced to migrate to Mars and have made Mars the home to a flourishing civilization. This advanced civilization, which was man-made comes suddenly under threat created by nature in the form of an asteroid of Jupiter. The asteroid from Jupiter was coming towards Mars and Mars was in danger of extinction. The scientists on Mars come up with a very innovative plan of a barrage of nuclear cannons to attack the oncoming asteroid. The bombardment destroys the asteroid and the year 3000 sees a Martian civilization surviving from the fury of the nature by scientific innovation. What a beautiful scientific thinking of Aardhra Krishna?

I was amazed about the poem written by a 12 year old girl Anna Sinyakova from Russia – "Never think of illness."

I always believed that there will be some problem or the other while doing important tasks, but problems should not become the master. My advice particularly to the young children is that you should defeat the problem and succeed. The same thoughts are echoed by Anna Sinyakova from Russia. She sends out a very strong message of encouragement and advice through her poem that you must have the courage to face any disease to keep up the human well-being.

I liked the painting of Savidhya Kumari Premasundera, a ten year old girl from Sri Lanka. The way she has imagined the scene of the fishing and the fishermen is testimony to the alertness and the observation capability of the young mind. Kenya's thirteen year old boy recounts his personal experience of his maiden flight which was hijacked. The entire incident had been so deeply engraved in the young mind. The boy has been very eloquent in bringing out his experiences and emotions in his write-up.

## Creativity can make Impossible Possible

According to the Laws of Aerodynamics, the shape of the bumble-bee is such that it should be impossible for it to fly. But the bee's determination to fly is strong. The bee keeps fluttering its wings and its life propels the bee. This high frequency vibration creates a vortex which enables it to fly. With determined efforts you can always succeed against established beliefs. That is the power of creativity.

Not only was the bumble-bee's flight, even the human flight considered impossible. In 1890, a well-known scientist, Lord Kelvin, who was the President of Royal Society of London, said that, "any thing heavier than air cannot fly, and cannot be flown." Two decades after that, the determination of the Wright Brothers made the impossible possible and proved that man could fly. Their success is a story of how sheer perseverance and creativity could lead to success.

This singular achievement has made the transportation revolution and made the world smaller.

The famous rocket designer Von Braun, built the Saturn-V to launch the capsule with astronauts and made moon walk a reality. He once said that, "If I am authorised, I will remove the word impossible", from the dictionary.

If you want to become a poet, writer or painter, you have to have a dream, and then acquire knowledge, work hard, you achieve the results as the bumble-bee, as the Wright Brothers, as the famous Indian scientists Sir C.V. Raman, as the painters like M.F. Hussian, Picasso, as a painter and sculptor like Amarnath Sehgal, as a poet like Rabindranath Tagore.

## Chandrayan Mission

Prof. Vikram Sarabhai gave a mission in the 1960s on what ISRO should do. He gave us a vision--that ISRO should design, develop and launch its own rockets, that is, satellite launch vehicles. It should launch communication satellites in geosynchronous orbits and remote-sensing satellites in polar sun-synchronous orbits. Both were needed for applications – to connect people through communication satellites, provide beneficial information to people and bring about connectivity State-to-State, and Country-to-Country. Remote-sensing spacecraft are intended to sense, to discover some of the natural wealth, forest wealth, and help in assessing the drought and flood condition.

ISRO has successfully realised Prof. Vikram Sarabhai's dream. What next? Now we have the Chandrayan programme, that is, orbiting a spacecraft around the moon. ISRO may land a small scientific payload on the Moon. In future we may go for Lunar Mining which could enable man to bring back to earth shipments of Helium-3, which is reported to be abundant on the moon, as a valuable fuel for thermonuclear reactors.

Now I would like to give you a ten point Oath.

**Conclusion: Ten Point Oath**

1. I will pursue my education or the work with dedication and I will excel in it.
2. From now onwards, I will teach at least 10 persons to read and write those who cannot read and write.
3. I will plant at least 10 saplings and shall ensure their growth through constant care.
4. I will visit rural and urban areas and permanently wean away at least 5 persons from addiction and gambling.
5. I will constantly endeavour to remove the pain of my suffering brethren.
6. I will not support any religious, caste or language differentiation.
7. I will be honest and endeavour to make a corruption-free society.
8. I will work for becoming an enlightened citizen and make my family righteous.
9. I will always be a friend of the mentally and physically challenged and will work hard to make them feel normal, like the rest of us.
10. I will proudly celebrate the success of my country and my people.

□

---

*Interaction with Shillong School Children, Raj Bhavan, Shillong on 23-09-2005.*

# 3

# The Design Teacher: Prof. Satish Dhawan

I worked in Delhi with the Ministry of Defence. Later I joined Defence Research and Development Organisation (DRDO) in 1958 at Aeronautical Development Establishment at Bangalore. There, I took up the development of Hovercraft. Hovercraft design needed the development of a ducted contra-rotating propeller for creating a smooth flow balancing the torques. I did not know how to design a contra-rotating propeller though I knew how to design a conventional propeller. Some of my friends told me that I can approach Prof. Satish Dhawan of Indian Institute of Science, Bengaluru, who was well-known for his aeronautical research, for help in designing the ducted contra-rotating propeller.

I took permission from my Director Dr. Mediratta and went to Prof. Satish Dhawan who was sitting in a small room in Indian Institute of Science with lot of books in the background and a blackboard on the wall. Prof. Satish Dhawan asked me what was the problem that I would like to discuss? I explained the problem to Prof. Dhawan about my project work. He told me that it is really a challenging task and he would teach me the design if I attend his classes in IISc between 2.00 p.m. to 3.00 p.m. on all Saturdays for the next six weeks. He was a visionary teacher. He prepared the schedule for the entire course and wrote it on the blackboard. He also gave me the reference material and books I should read before I start attending the course. I considered, this as a great opportunity and I started attending the discussion and started meeting him regularly. Before commencing each meeting, he would ask critical questions and assess my understanding of the subject. That was for the first time that I realised how a good teacher prepares himself for teaching with meticulous planning and prepares the student for acquisition of knowledge. This process continued for the next six weeks. I got the capability for designing the contra-rotating propeller. Prof. Dhawan told me that I am ready for developing the contra-rotating propeller for a given hovercraft configuration. That was the time I realised that Prof. Satish Dhawan was not only a teacher but also a fantastic development engineer of aeronautical systems.

Later during the critical phases of testing Professor Dhawan was with me to witness the test and found solutions to the problems. After reaching the smooth test phase, contra-rotating propeller went through 50 hours of continuous testing. Prof. Satish Dhawan witnessed the test himself and congratulated me. That was a great day for me when I saw the contra-rotating propeller designed by my team performing to the mission requirement in the hovercraft. However, at that time, I did not realize that Prof. Satish Dhawan would become the Chairman of Indian Space Research Organisation (ISRO) and that I would get the opportunity to work with him as a Project Director in the development of first satellite launch vehicle SLV-3 for injecting the Rohini Satellite into the orbit. Nature has its own way to link the student's dream and the real life later.

Design of contra-rotating propeller was the first project in my career which gave me the confidence to design many complex aerospace systems in future. The hovercraft could fly just above the ground level carrying two passengers. I was the first pilot for this hovercraft and I could control and manoeuvre the vehicle in any direction. Through this project I learnt the techniques of designing and developing the contra-rotating propeller. Above all, I learnt that in a project, problems will always crop up; we should not allow problems to be our masters but we should defeat the problems. The lessons that I learnt from Prof. Satish Dhawan for the next four decades are: the importance of design capability and the need for indomitable spirit.

**Employment Generation through Entrepreneurship**

There has been substantial growth in our educational system and we are generating over 3 million graduates every year and another 7 million educated upto 10 or 10+2 level. However, our employment generation system is not in a position to absorb the graduates passing out from the universities leading to increase in educated unemployed, year after year. This situation will lead to instability in the social structure. We need education integrated with an entrepreneurial spirit. A multi pronged strategy is needed to make education more attractive and simultaneously create employment potential? How do we do that?

Firstly, the educational system should highlight the importance of entrepreneurship and prepare the students right from the school and college education to get oriented towards setting up of the enterprises which will provide them creativity, freedom and ability to generate wealth. Apart from entrepreneurship, the youth should have the spirit that? We can do it? Secondly, the banking system should provide venture capital right from every village level to the prospective entrepreneurs for undertaking new enterprises. Banks have to be proactive to support the innovative products for enabling wealth generation by young entrepreneurs by setting aside the conventional tangible asset syndrome? Definitely this involves certain amount of calculated risks which can be eliminated by making an analysis of successful venture capital enterprises. Thirdly, there is a need to identify marketable products and enhancement of purchasing power among the people. This can come through the implementation of mega programmes such as rural prosperity through connectivity (RUPCON), Interlinking of Rivers, Infrastructure missions, Power missions and Tourism.

The universities should become a facilitator for creating this entrepreneurship scheme through the support of the banking system and the marketing system. This is one way of reducing the employment gap leading to upliftment of the 260 million people living below the poverty line.

## An Island Transforming into a Missile Launch Complex

I was working in India's missile programme during 1982 to 1999. Even though my place of work was Hyderabad, my theatre of action was always Chandipur and Wheeler Islands of Orissa coast where the developed missiles were flight tested. I would like to narrate an interesting experience which happened during that period.

In October 1993, the development of Prithvi missile was almost over. However, the Army desired to have a confirmatory test, on a land range, to validate the Circular Error Probability (CEP) of the missile. Our efforts to conduct the tests in our desert range could not take off due to range safety problems. To overcome this we were looking for an uninhabited island in the Eastern coast. On the hydrographic map supplied by Navy, we saw a few islands in the Bay of Bengal off Dhamra (Orissa coast) indicating that there was some land mass. Our range team consisting of Dr. S.K. Salwan and Shri V.K. Saraswat hired a boat from Dhamra and went in search of the island. On the map these islands were marked as long wheeler coconut wheeler and small wheeler. The team carried a directional compass and proceeded on the journey. They lost their way and could not locate the Wheeler Island. Fortunately, they met few fishing boats and asked them for the route. The fisherman did not know about the Wheeler Island but they said there was an Island called Chandrachood. They thought that this could be the Wheeler Island. They approximately gave the direction for proceeding to Chandrachood. With this help the team could reach the Chandrachood Island, which was later confirmed as Small Wheeler Island. By this time it was late in the evening and it was dark.

The boatman refused to move in the night and the team had to stay in the Small Wheeler Island in the boat for the night counting the stars. Next morning the team came back to Dhamra. On physical survey of the three Islands it was found that the long wheeler island had eroded over a period of time and was not useful for range activities. In view of this we chose small wheeler, which had adequate width and length required for range operations. The team also found some signs of boats from other countries visiting the small wheeler island. A study of the hydrographic data of number of years indicated the erosion characteristic of the island. After taking over the islands from the Orissa Government for range activities, we created permanent stony bunds on the periphery of the selected islands to prevent the future erosion. This one tiny island has been transformed into a world class missile range complex. What we learn from this experience is: aim great missions, work for it and you will achieve.

## Wealth Generation Through Biodiversity

Western Orissa is bestowed with rich tropical forest resource and it is the store house of medicinal plants in the Gandhamardan hill areas. Also I understand that Sambalpur University has a well equipped life science department and many others. A nation's strength predominantly resides in its natural and human resources. In natural resources, India is endowed with a vast coastline with marine resources. India ranks among the top few nations having a rich biodiversity. Particularly, in the herbal area there are potential applications for developing multiple products for nutrition, prevention and cure of diseases. There are tremendous opportunities for growth in global market of herbal product. India has similar potential for promoting floriculture and aquaculture in a big way. India is rich in herbs, germ plasm and microorganisms. Industrially developed countries are importing these bioresources in the raw forms and add value to them for export to developing countries including India as special seeds, medicines and biomaterials, fully protecting patents of these products. Instead of allowing export of such resources and importing value-added products at high cost, India must add its own technology for conversion of such resources to value-added products for use in domestic requirement and also for export. Use of IT for commercialization and marketing can increase our outreach and speed enormously. Ancient knowledge is a unique resource of India, for it has the treasure of more than 5000 years of civilization. In Rashtrapati Bhavan a herbal garden has been developed with 32 varieties of plants particularly Geranium, Sadabahar and Sarpagandha, which attracts a large number of young researchers, farmers, small-scale entrepreneurs, industrialists and students.

## Conclusion

I have discussed here my experiences with a design teacher, employment generation through entrepreneurship, an island transforming into a launch complex and wealth generation through biodiversity. These experiences emphasize the importance of indomitable spirit in realizing any mission leading to progress of individuals.

Development is dynamic; it is a vibrant continuum; it is a multifaceted phenomenon. It is essential to grasp the real concept of development to ensure holistic growth and full realization of goals. As we move towards the development of Orissa with economic strength, competitiveness, knowledge power and technology, productivity needs, effective governance and empowered management, we also need invisible leadership. Invisible leaders are those, whose leadership styles move from commander to coach, manager to mentor, from director to delegator and from one who demands respect to one who facilitates self-respect.

□

*Address at the 21st Convocation of Sambalpur University, Sambalpur on 04-06-2004.*

# 4

# Indian Science Inspire Youth?

## International Year of Physics – 2005

One of the major breakthroughs in science in the 20th century that had an everlasting impact on the human kind is the most celebrated work of Einstein. Einstein explained, for the first time in 1905, the principle of the inertia of energy as a universal law. The famous energy equation $E = MC^2$ was given to the world. This equation has become the basis for converting matter into energy giving birth to a new avenue called the nuclear energy for producing electricity to light up our cities and villages. Science at times is a double-edged sword. While the $E=MC^2$ of Einstein, changed the way the humanity looked at the energy problem, it also paved the way for the design of Atom bomb. The latter application even today threatens to disturb the world peace. In spite of this, Einstein's work is most profound and opened up many areas of research and development in physics. The scientific community of the world decided to pay tribute to Einstein by declaring the year 2005 as the International Year of Physics. India will celebrate Einstein's anniversary by paying special attention to basic sciences in our schools and colleges, modernizing and reforming our institutions of science and, above all, re-dedicating itself to the spread of scientific temper. When I think of Einstein, I am reminded of the observation made by him about our father of the nation, Mahatma Gandhi, Generations to come will scarcely believe that such one as this (Gandhiji) ever in flesh and blood walked upon this earth?

## Raman Effect

Raman is one of the greatest scientists that India ever produced. Raman was extremely creative even with inexpensive equipments and in simple environments. One of his notable contributions to science is the discovery of what later came to be known as 'Raman Effect'. Raman Effect is the appearance of additional lines in the spectrum of monochromatic light that has been scattered by a transparent material medium. Sir C.V. Raman discovered the effect in 1928. The energy and thus the frequency and the wavelength of the scattered light are changed as the light either imparts rotational or vibrational energy to the scattering molecules or takes energy away. The line spectrum of the scattered light will have one prominent line corresponding to the original wavelength of the incident radiation, plus additional lines to each side of it corresponding to the shorter or longer wavelengths of the altered portion of the light. This Raman spectrum is the unique characteristic of the material medium. Thus, Raman spectrometry is a useful technique in physical and chemical research, particularly for the characterization of materials.

This in-elastically scattered light is called 'Raman Scatter'. Energy difference between incident light and the Raman scattered light is equal to the energy involved in changing the molecule vibrational state. The Raman Effect is useful in the study of molecular energy levels, structure development and multicomponent qualitative analysis.

Raman Effect has continuously impacted every field of science. Its role in spectroscopy, medical diagnostics and material characterization had been phenomenal. The Raman Effect had been used in many new areas of science and the most recent being in the development of a continuous silicon laser. Instruments and techniques based on Raman Effect make a huge industry all over the world.

In a paper published February 17, 2005 in Nature, Intel researchers disclosed the development of the first continuous wave all-silicon laser using the Raman Effect. They built the experimental device using the standard CMOS manufacturing processes.

Intel researchers incorporated a novel diode-like structure into the silicon cavity laser. This diode combined with the Raman Effect produces a continuous laser beam at a new wavelength. This breakthrough device could lead to many practical applications such as optical amplifiers, lasers, wavelength converters, and new kinds of high efficient optical devices. A low-cost all-silicon Raman laser could inspire innovation in the development of new medical sensors, and spectroscopy devices.

Over the next 5 to 10 years, the computing and communications industries would face increasing challenges to deliver more data and faster. Consumers will be downloading full-length movies, not just photos and music files. People will also require faster access to these large amounts of data. While microprocessors are projected to meet these future demands, the bandwidth of the interconnects needs to be increased to meet the speed of the microprocessors. With the new work of Intel using Raman Effect to produce continuous silicon laser, the material convergence will take place very soon and faster networks would emerge.

## Birth of Triple Helix

Dr. G.N. Ramachandran known as GNR amongst scientists is great Indian scientist. His life is indeed an example worthy of emulation by all scientists, which was a fusion of curiosity, creativity and problem solving ability for successful missions. GNR, was wondering how to go about with x-ray diffraction and X-ray crystallography base with application to biomolecules as a main theme. J.D. Bernal, the famous crystallographer and chemist who was on a visit to India in 1942 felt that all the structure proposed so far for collagen were unsatisfactory and suggested that GNR could take a look at that. How to get collagen was indeed a big problem for GNR at that time. He presented his problem to Dr. Nayudamma, the then Director of CLRI, Madras. Within a few days, Dr. Nayudamma procured a tube full of collagen from Australia. This helped GNR to publish the first innovative paper on the collagen structure, which gave strikingly original triple helix it appeared in the journal *Nature* in August 7, 1954. The proposed structure consisted of three separate helical chains, with their axis parallel to the fiber axis, stacked in a hexagonal array. This structure was not only innovative, it also provided better quantitative agreement with the X-ray data. Collagen is today finding large-scale application in the treatment of third degree burn injuries, since it has been found to have extraordinary healing properties. Also collagen has led to a separate branch of biology named structural biology, which is being taught in many universities. GNR can rightly be called as the father of structural biology. The world will always be thankful to him, for giving the famous Ramachandran plot.

## The Glorious Phase of Indian Science

In India, science and technology in the pre-independent era, specifically starting from the thirties was influenced by the six great scientists of international repute. They are Sir, C.V. Raman, Prof. Chandrasekhar Subramaniam, S.N. Bose, J.C. Bose, Meghnad Saha and Srinivasa Ramanujam. This phase, I consider the glorious phase of Indian science. The scientific foundation laid by them always stimulated the later generations also. This was also the beginning of the emergence of a confident India, in spite of her subjugation. The second phase is the post independent phase of science and technology in India.

## The Post-independence Phase of Indian Science and Technology

In history, any country revolves itself initially around a few stout and earnest knowledge giants. Particularly I took interest to study lives of three scientists, as I was interested in their scientific technological leadership qualities that focused the relationship of S&T and development of the nation. In the history of India, there may be many but I was very close to these three great personalities for one reason or the other. They are founders of three great institutions. I worked in two of the institutions directly and one in partnership. Dr. D.S. Kothari, a Professor in Delhi University was an outstanding Physicist and also an Astrophysicist. He is well-known for ionization of matter by pressure in cold compact objects like planets. This theory is complementary to thermal ionization work done by Dr. Meghnad Saha his Guru. Dr. D.S. Kothari set a scientific tradition in Indian defence tasks when he became Scientific Adviser to Defence Minister in 1948; He created a Board of Advisors to the Scientific Advisor consisting of Dr. H.J. Bhabha, Dr. K.S. Krishnan and Dr. S.S. Bhatnagar. Later the Board was renamed as Scientific Advisory Board with enlarged membership.

He established the Defence Science Centre to do research in electronic material, nuclear medicine and ballistic science. He is considered as the architect of defence science in India. His race continued and followed up with momentum working and contributing in the areas of strategic systems, electronic warfare systems, armaments and life sciences.

## Pioneer in Indian Nuclear Science (Homi Jahangir Bhabha)

Homi Jahangir Bhabha did research in theoretical physics in Cambridge University. During 1930-1939, Homi Bhabha carried out research relating to cosmic radiation.

In 1939, he joined Sir C.V. Raman in IISc Bangalore. Later, he was asked to start the Tata Institute of Fundamental Research with focus on nuclear science, mathematical science and established Atomic Energy Commission in 1948. Multi centers were born with his vision in nuclear science to nuclear technology, nuclear power, nuclear devices and nuclear medicine. These science institutions established multi technological centers, but basic science is the vital component.

## Indian Space Visionary

Thirdly Prof. Vikram Sarabhai was my Guru, the youngest of the three and worked with Sri C.V. Raman in experimental cosmic ray research. Prof. Sarabhai established Physical Research Laboratory (PRL) Ahmedabad with Space Research as focus. PRL was the cradle of Indian Space Programme. In later years he became the Director of Space S&T Centre. The SSTC (1963) started with launching sounding rockets for space atmospheric research. Prof. Vikram Sarabhai unfurled the space mission for India in 1970 that we should build Satellite Launch Vehicle capability, to put our communication satellites in the geo-synchronous orbit and remote sensing satellites in the polar orbit. Also, he envisaged that launch vehicles built in India should be launched from Indian soil. This one visionary thought led to intensive research and development in multiple fields of science and space technology. Many of us had the fortune to be part of Prof. Vikram Sarabhai's vision. Myself and my team participated in India's first satellite launch vehicle programme to put the satellite in the orbit. Today, India with her 20,000 scientific, technological and support staff in multiple space research centres, supported by about 300 industries and academic institutions, has the capability to build any type of satellite launch vehicle to place remote sensing, communication and meteorology satellites in different orbits and space application has become part of our daily life.

## Scientific Excellence in India

I have discussed the great tradition of science, particularly physics on the day of discovery of Raman Effect. It is important for us. There are 100s of scientific laboratories, and R&D Institutions in space, defence and many other areas and a number of universities. It is time that our scientific, technological academic institutions and universities should carry out an internal review and assess for themselves where do they stand in relation to academic institutions of excellence in the world.

## Biopesticide Development

First I would like to discuss about biopesticide development. Development of safe and sustainable alternatives to chemical insecticides is absolutely essential as it has become a liability for good soil. A research mission has been taken up by International Centre for Genetic Engineering and Bio-technology to isolate a bacterium from soil dwelling nematode, which is highly pathogenic to insects. Sustained research and field trials during the last two years, at various locations in the country, of the formulation consisting of bacterium has led to successful optimised formulation resulting in a viable biopesticide. As reported, the formulation is effective in agricultural and horticultural insect pests like diamond back moth of cabbage and cauliflower, mealy bugs of citrus fruits and grapes and termites in teak plantation. White woolly aphid of sugar cane, which is a major factor in reducing the sugar production of Maharashtra, Karnataka and Andhra Pradesh, is effectively controlled by the biopesticide. Its efficacy is comparable to the chemical insecticide. This scientific research leading to technology has been transferred to a start up biotech company Nirmal Seeds Ltd. and it is marketed under the brand name, BIO PRAHAR. I am sure that this work will lead to improved food productivity in a very eco-friendly way.

## Drug for Faster Cure of Tuberculosis

Second achievement is the development of a drug for faster cure of tuberculosis. Modern medicine has always relied on newer scientific discoveries world over. Indian scientific research starts to focus in finding solutions to our problems, which can later on be applied to the people of other countries. In this regard, India has made a very significant contribution in developing a drug uniquely suitable for Indian ambiance. One of the achievements comes from a laboratory of (CSIR), the Council of Scientific and Industrial Research. CSIR lab has developed a new therapeutic molecule for Tuberculosis. This molecule has shown the potential to cure TB in around 2 months, as against the standard treatment of 6 to 8 months. This breakthrough is very important as we have number of TB patients. After completing the pre-clinical studies, the molecule transformed into a drug is planned to undergo clinical trials in humans. It is commendable that the entire development has been done as a public-private partnership involving the Lupin, the three CSIR Laboratories, namely, Central Drug Research Institute, Indian Institute of Chemical Technology and National Chemical Laboratory, and the University of Hyderabad.

## Nanotube Filter – Water Purification

Third achievement is the development of a nano-tube filter. The scientists from Banaras Hindu University have devised a simple method to produce carbon nanotube filters that efficiently remove micro- to nano-scale contaminants from water and heavy hydrocarbons from petroleum. Made entirely of carbon nanotubes, the filters are easily manufactured using a novel method for controlling the cylindrical geometry of the structure. The work was supported in part by the Ministry of Human Resources Development and Department of Science and Technology in India.

The filters are hollow carbon cylinders several centimeters long and one or two centimeters wide with walls just one-third to one-half a millimeter thick. They are produced by spraying benzene into a tube-shaped quartz mold and heating the mold to 900°C. The nano-tube composition makes the filters strong, reusable, and heat resistant, and they can be cleaned easily for reuse. The carbon nanotube filters offer a level of precision suitable for different applications. The experiments demonstrated that the filters may be useful in producing high-octane gasoline. They also can remove 25-nanometer-sized polio viruses from water, as well as larger pathogens, such as *E. coli* and Staphylococcus aaureus bacteria. The researchers believe this could make the filters adaptable to microfluidics applications that separate chemicals in drug discovery.

This is a classic application of the latest in science – Nano science, to age-old problem of water purification. If properly used, this can help in lessoning the burden in our drinking water missions leading to the availability of safe drinking water that will result in minimizing the water-borne diseases.

## Gene Chip

Fourth area is Gene Chip for curing heart diseases. Cardiomyopathy means "Diseases of the heart muscle," which leads to heart failure or sudden death. There are 3 main types: Dilated, hypertrophic or restrictive Cardiomyopathy. It progresses since childhood and the onset of the disease vary according to the family history. Although transplantation may be an effective strategy in these patients, its implementation is hindered by availability of donor as well as numerous ethical, social, economic and legal issues. Similarly the mechanical cardiac assist devices are also not cost-effective for long-term usage in our population.

The Human Genome Project has increased the impact of genetics in medical science and practice. Genetics of Cardiomyopathy remain unknown. Also, the molecular etiology is not known in many cases of Cardiomyopathies affecting children as well as adults, with an annual incidence of 2-8 per 10,000 in the United States and Europe. Though there are reports on association of mutations in nuclear genome and Cardiomyopathy, quite a number of cases do not show any such mutations. As there is a close relationship with the cardiac muscle contraction and energy metabolism, it is quite reasonable to speculate the role of mitochondrial DNA variations as possible cause of these cases. Recent reports have shown evidence in support of the role of mitochondrial mutation in the pathogenesis of Cardiomyopathies in western population. There is no large sample study have been carried out so far to find molecular etiology of Cardiomyopathy in Indian population.

The scientists from International Centre for Biomedical Sciences and Technology (Research and Applications), have reported several novel mutations that could be the possible cause of the disease, and some pathogenic mutations whose role is proved in other mitochondrial diseases, by sequencing the 5 unrelated individuals with severe Cardiomyopathies. This is the first report of the mitochondrial DNA analysis of the cardiac patients from the Indian subcontinent. Fortunately the administering stem cell has found cure in AIIMS for the specific type of Cardiomyopathy.

**Novel Detection Kit for HIV/AIDS**

Fifth Area is about the development of a novel detection kit, NEVA-HIV to detect HIV (AIDS) in a drop of blood within three minutes. It is a single step test in which a drop of blood is mixed with a drop of a reagent on a glass slide. If the blood sample shows clumping, it is positive for HIV. This clumping of blood can be easily seen with the naked eye, hence the test is called the Naked Eye Visible Agglutination assay or NEVA. This test uses recombinant proteins consisting of a monovalent fragment of an anti-human RBC monoclonal antibody fused to a specific protein antigen derived from HIV. These proteins cross-link RBCs in the presence of anti-HIV antibodies, which are present in the blood of HIV infected individuals. The test uses recombinant proteins consisting of NEVA-HIV is one of the very few tests in the world that can be performed on whole blood, even from a finger prick. Developed, keeping in mind the practical constraints of HIV testing in our country, NEVA-HIV is an instrument-free test. In addition, the simplicity and rapidity of the test, makes it suitable for use in a primary health centre of a village even in a remote part of our country.

The test has been evaluated at several national reference centres and has been found to have high sensitivity and specificity. This novel scientific development has been carried out by the faculty members of Department of Biochemistry, University of Delhi in collaboration with the Department of Biotechnology and Cadila Pharmaceuticals Ltd., Ahmedabad.

## Binary Millisecond Pulsar

Sixth area is the discovery of binary millisecond pulsar. A pulsar is the remnant of a star which exploded, leaving behind a sphere made up of neutrons just 20 kms in size but weighing more than the sun. The pulsar emits a beam of radio waves which is seen from the earth as a pulse every time it rotates. These waves are very weak, when they reach the earth. In order to detect the pulsar, one needs the Giant Metrewave Radio Telescope (GMRT). The Tata Institute of Fundamental Research (TIFR) has built the largest Radio telescope in the world in rural area near the village of Khodad, 80 km from Pune. Because of the unique capabilities of our GMRT, scientist from all over the world including USA and Canada visit the Centre to conduct collaborative experiments. Our scientists played a leading role in the recent discovery of a new, 'Binary millisecond pulsar'. Astronomy had been the strong point of ancient Indian science. Discoveries like the one that has been made by the scientists of the National Centre for Radio Astrophysics of TIFR, is an important contribution for Indian science.

## Conclusion

A nation of billion people will certainly have many more achievements that will justify her being ranked third in the world in terms of scientific manpower. The six illustrations, I gave above, are more to show that the Indian science is in the ascending trajectory. The Indian science fabric is very vast and all encompassing. The Indian science awaits all of you, youth to join her in the journey of progress and excitement. Definitely Indian science particularly the experience of experienced scientists should be available to inspire the youth who aspire to take up science as their mission.

Science has helped us to increase food productivity, create the white and green revolution, improve communication, produce electricity using nuclear science, enhance the quality of life, attempt novel things of use to humanity and leading us towards a healthier and happy nation. Thanks to science we live longer, have reduced infant deaths, and have overcome diseases more effectively. When I was a child one of the dreaded disease in India was smallpox. It hit every village and town killed millions and left millions with pockmarks on their faces. Science came to our rescue. Now smallpox is history, a disease of the past.

Can we apply science to eradicate the poverty, remove illiteracy, make all Indians healthy and make it a partner in generating wealth to the nation for transforming India into a developed nation by the year 2020. The answer to the question is 'Yes', since the development of the nation has to be done through application of technology since nonlinear growth can only be achieved through technology. The development of technology needs science. If we desire to nurture the nation, we have to nurture science and scientists. Let us all work together to promote a scientific temper among our youth who are the greatest partners in the transformation process.

□

---

*Address to the Nation by the President of India on the Science Day 2005, New Delhi on 28-02-2005.*

# 5

# The Vision of India

Indian civilizational heritage is built on universal spirit. India always stood for friendship and extends warm hands to the whole world. We have made significant achievements in the last fifty years in food production, health sector, higher education, media and mass communication, industrial infrastructure, information technology, science and technology and defence. Our nation is endowed with natural resources, vibrant people and traditional value system. In spite of these resources, a number of our people are below the poverty line, undernourished and lack primary education itself. Our aim is to empower them to be poverty free, healthy and literate. A country needs to have the characteristics as defined in Thirukkural, composed over 2000 years ago:

"The important elements that constitute a nation are: being disease free; wealth; high productivity; harmonious living and strong defence." All our efforts should be focused towards building these five elements at various levels in a coherent and in an integrated manner. I am convinced that our nation with a strong, vibrant and billion plus population can contribute to realize these elements.

Today our country is facing challenges such as cross border terrorism, certain internal conflicts and un-employment. To face these challenges, there must be a vision to ensure focused action of one billion citizens of this great country with varied capabilities. What can be that vision? It can be none other than transforming India into a 'Developed Nation'. Can government alone achieve this Vision? Now, we need a movement in the country. This is the time to ignite the minds of the people for this movement. We will work for it. We cannot emerge as a developed nation if we do not learn to transact with speed. I recall the saintly poet Kabir's wisdom to us:

"What you want to do tomorrow do it today, and what you want to do today do it now."

This vision of developed nation needs to be achieved with Parliamentary democracy, which is the core of our governance system. The basic structure of our Constitution has stood the test of time. I am confident that it will continue to be responsive to the demands of changing situations. The first and foremost task is to respect and uphold the constitutional processes, in the best interest of our people and our nation, without fear or favour and with fairness and firmness. India is a Union of States based on the framework of cooperative federalism. Within the cooperative framework, there is also a requirement to develop competitive strengths for the States so that they can excel at the national level and the global level. Competitiveness helps in ensuring economic and managerial efficiency and to be creative to meet new challenges. These are essential to survive and prosper in a fast changing world of today. In addition, in order to strengthen democratic processes and institution, we should all truly strive for substantive decentralization.

I emphasize my unflinching commitment to the principle of secularism, which is the cornerstone of our nationhood and which is the key feature of our civilisational strength. I met a number of spiritual leaders of all religions. They all echoed one message, that is, unity of minds and hearts of our people will happen and we will see the golden age of our country, very soon. I would like to endeavour to work for bringing about unity of minds among the divergent traditions of our country.

Along with speedy development aimed at elimination of poverty and un-employment, national security has to be recognised by every Indian as a national priority. Indeed, making India strong and self-reliant – economically, socially and militarily – is our foremost duty to our motherland and to ourselves and to our future generations.

When the child is empowered by the parents, at various phases of growth, the child transforms into a responsible citizen. When the teacher is empowered with knowledge and experience, good young human beings with value systems take shape. When individual or a team is empowered with technology, transformation to higher potential for achievement is assured. When the leader of any institution empowers his or her people, leaders are born who can change the nation in multiple areas. When the women are empowered, society with stability gets assured. When the political leaders of the nation empower the people through visionary policies, the prosperity of the nation is certain. The medium for transformation to developed India is the empowerment at various levels with power of knowledge. A roadmap for realizing this vision of developed India is in front of us.

At this juncture, I recall a beautiful thought of Dr. G.G. Swell, an eminent leader from North-East: "We must have a mental infrastructure. Mental infrastructure means sincerity of purpose, of vision, of purity of heart and mind."

When I travel across our nation, when I hear the sound of waves of the three seas around the shores of my country, when I experience the breeze of wind from the mighty Himalayas, when I see the biodiversity of North-East and our islands and when I feel the warmth from the western desert, I hear the voice of the youth. "When can I sing the song of India?" If youth have to sing the song of India, India should become a developed country which is free from poverty, illiteracy and un-employment and is buoyant with economic prosperity, national security and internal harmony. To create this transformation we all have to resolve ourselves to work and sweat for the national development. I would like to share the song of youth, which I normally recite with the school children, here at this juncture. I am very happy to see the children present here representing the future generation. Through them I would like to convey the song of youth to all children of our country and the people.

As a young citizen of India, armed with technology, knowledge and love for my nation, I realize, small aim is a crime.

I will work and sweat for a great vision, the vision of transforming India into a developed nation, powered by economic strength with value system.

I am one of the citizens of the billion; Only the vision will ignite the billion souls.

It has entered into me; The ignited soul compared to any resource is the most powerful resource on the earth, above the earth and under the earth.

I will keep the lamp of knowledge burning to achieve the vision – Developed India.

If we work and sweat for the great vision with ignited minds, the transformation leading to the birth of vibrant developed India will happen. This song, when sung in our own beautiful languages will unite our minds for action.

"May the divine peace with beauty enter into our people; Happiness and good health blossom in our bodies, minds and souls."

□

---

*Assumption of Office as President of India, New Delhi on 25-07-2002.*

# 6

# What should We be Remembered For?

Let us for a moment pause to reflect what it is that for which we would like to be remembered for by future generations. Will we be remembered for how many mosques our generation has added, will we be remembered for how many temples our generation has added or will we be remembered for how many *gurudwaras* our generation has added?

No, not at all. We will be remembered only if we give to our younger generation a prosperous and safe India, resulting out of economic prosperity coupled with civilisational heritage.

At this point of time I would like to share with you an experience, which I had at Raj Bhavan, Srinagar during my recent visit to the three regions of Jammu and Kashmir. A number of children from different schools of the city and the neighbourhood interacted with me and sang with me the National Anthem.

At the end of our interaction, three students approached me and introduced themselves. One was a Hindu girl, the second a Muslim boy and the third a Sikh boy. They asked me: 'Mr President, please tell us now, when will we become prosperous, free from poverty and from the fear of terrorist attacks? Allow us to go on a mission to penetrate the minds of the extremists and bring about unity of minds.'

These children represent the 300 million strong youth of the nation. The questions of the students engulfed me, resulting in a poetic verse.

'Oh Almighty, create thoughts and actions in the minds of the people of my nation, so that they live united. Light the minds of the religious leaders of my country to evolve a bridge among religions, with compassion and love'.

Embed the thought 'Nation is bigger than the individual or party!' in the minds of the leaders.

## Aspirations of the People

I interacted with various cross-sections of the people and had an exclusive dialogue with Members of Parliament and legislators of certain states and also presented the Developed India Plan to the Joint Session of Parliament.

The dialogue with the people, and written responses from many citizens gave me an insight into the aspirations of the people to get into the action of transforming India into a developed nation, in less than two decades. Whether it was a remote village in Kerala, or a far away rural set-up in Nagaland or Uri in Jammu and Kashmir, the area close to the Line of Control, I would like to emphatically state that the feelings and aspirations for a prosperous India are the same.

## Our Strengths

For India to become a developed nation, we must give thrust to the nation's core competencies. The GDP has to grow annually by 8 to 10 per cent with consistency over years instead of the current 5 per cent. This year, it is reassuring that our economy in three sectors – agriculture, manufacturing and services is in the ascent phase. If we put in united efforts to keep up the momentum we can reach an 8 per cent growth rate in about a year. We should ensure the benefits of this growth should reach the economically weaker sections of society.

We should reinforce our gains in the agriculture, power, Information and Communication Technology, industrial and education sectors, space, nuclear, and defence technologies, chemical, pharmaceutical and infrastructural industries, oil exploration and refining, and more importantly in critical technologies.

When we are consolidating our strengths, we should develop increased safety consciousness to prevent loss of valuable human and material resources in road, rail, air, power, industrial and other accidents. The relief mechanisms have to reach accident sites at the right time.

The core competencies, resources and safety consciousness should be the basis on which the country can embark on a national mission for transformation.

## Vision to Mission

We need to evolve and develop specific integrated missions sector-wise to take the country forward on the path of self-sustaining development. These missions will provide the thrust for the realisation of a developed India in a time bound manner. They will also provide large-scale employment opportunities for the youth, through the creation of various types of industries and enhancement of national infrastructure. I would like to discuss five specific missions.

## Networking of Rivers

The first mission on the Networking of Rivers is under active consideration of my government and from the task team evolving the plan of action, we must move on to a mission mode programme including an ecological enhancement plan for executing the project. This mission will eliminate the periodical problem of droughts and floods experienced in a number of river basin states and provide both water and power security. In addition the nation has to embark on water harvesting and desalination of seawater as national missions.

## Quality Power

Availability of quality uninterrupted power should be ensured at an affordable price, which is a key to economic growth. This is our second mission. The existing capacity of about 100,000 megawatts would need tripling by the year 2020. To achieve it, apart from hydel, thermal and nuclear power systems, we need to give thrust to sustainable energy resources like biomass, wind and solar farms of 800 to 1000 megawatts capacity and to efficient transmission and distribution.

## Providing Urban amenities in Rural Areas (PURA)

Providing urban facilities to rural areas is another important mission. In the long-term interest, it is necessary for us to make living in villages an attractive proposition for our people by reinforcing the rural habitat and providing modern economic linkages. To achieve this, an economically viable cluster of villages have to be created through a mission mode programme into physical, electronic, and knowledge connectivities, leading to self-sustained economic prosperity for groups of villages. It is essential that PURA has to become a business proposition to be run by small-scale industrialists, entrepreneurs, and societal establishments.

## Information and Communication Technology (ICT)

The mission of Information and Communication Technology (ICT) and related services is one of the wealth generators for the nation. We should aspire to increase business volume by 15 to 20 times in a ten-year duration.

The benefit of ICT must reach all parts of the country through telemedicine, teleeducation and e-governance.

We have to embark on creating ICT infrastructure and developing knowledge products to promote selective self-reliance in the ICT sector, thus achieving a competitive edge globally.

## Tourism

The vast civilisational heritage of the country, from the Himalayas to Kanyakumari, Jammu and Kashmir, central India, the North-Eastern States, Bihar, the western states, the large coastal line, the Andaman and Nicobar Islands and Lakshadweep Islands have a lot to attract tourists. After my visit to almost all the regions of the country, I have realised the tourism industry has a tremendous potential for wealth generation and should operate as our fifth mission with higher targets.

To succeed in this mission, infrastructural requirements are very essential and are to be improved. Thrust is required to be given for inland water navigation, hotels, communications and tourist promotion. If we promote sustainable tourism, it will become India's core competence. These mission areas need action and will provide a multiplier effect and give the necessary momentum to all sectors of the economy.

## Enriching Village Life

During my visit to rural areas in certain States, I realised that the hard earned money of rural people, instead of being deployed for education of children and environmental improvements including their habitat, was being wasted in undesirable practices like alcoholism and other addictions. In certain states, I realised the ratio between males and females was not proportionate. This prompted me to evolve a declaration in consultation with the rural population for administering it to village life is as follows:

- Children are our precious wealth.

- We will give equal importance to male and female children in providing education and rights for growth of our society.
- Earnings come out of hard work. We will not waste it in gambling and liquor. We will become role models for kids.
- We need to tell our children about the importance of education as learning gives knowledge.
- We need to jointly protect our forests and prevent pollution.
- We will plant at least five trees or saplings.

It is essential that reputed leaders and social workers while visiting rural areas can administer this oath in a similar way. Social workers, women self-help groups and non-governmental organisations have to take-up this task as a mission. For India to develop we need vibrant villages.

## Challenges

Divisive forces use terrorism as a tool in the name of ethnic groupism, religious fundamentalism and sometimes political ambitions as a rationale for terrorism, leading to conflicts among nations. People are used as war tools. Within the next two decades, we will encounter a totally new situation of acute shortages of water, energy and minerals.

No single nation will be able to handle this situation by itself. Humanity will require mega-missions for harnessing solar energy, drinking water from seawater through the desalination process and bringing minerals from other planets. In such a situation, the present reasons for conflict will become insignificant and unwarranted. Our neighbouring countries have to see this perspective and have a bigger vision. India has definitely taken a significant peace initiative with all its neighbours.

The recent visit of our Prime Minister to China definitely paves the way for resolving certain outstanding issues.

The recent terrorist attack in Jammu and Kashmir and other states through a suicide bombing, resulting in a number of casualties, of both service and civilian personnel, is a cause for serious concern. No religion has mandated killing others as a requirement for its sustenance or promotion. These cowardly acts borne out of utter frustration deserve severe condemnation and actions for preventing recurrence of such events.

## Tasks Before Us

Developed India 2020 vision transforming into a mission is a national challenge and requires nationwide participation. While my government is committed for such missions, every citizen of India should ask in what way he or she can contribute to these missions directly or indirectly. It is difficult to spell out all specific possibilities of tangible contribution by our citizens. I would like to mention a few here, as examples:

Educationists should build the capacities of the spirit of inquiry, creativity, entrepreneurial and moral leadership among students and become their role model. Today, professional education is becoming a commercial venture. It is not affordable for even middle class people, what to talk of people below the poverty line, state governments, universities and the managements of educational institutions should review and streamline the procedural and systemic bottlenecks in executing missions. Actions emanating from the government in all its public dealings should become fully transparent through e-governance.

Parliamentarians and legislators belonging to each constituency should become mission facilitators for their constituency and also resolve inter and intra-constituency conflicts. I am reminded of a Talim epic, which provides the code of conduct for people in high and responsible positions.

It means, people who are in high and responsible positions, if they go against righteousness, righteousness itself will get transformed into a destroyer. Whoever deviates from righteousness, whether they are an individual or states, are responsible for their own actions.

If a country is to be corruption free and become a nation of beautiful minds, I strongly feel there are three key societal members who can make a difference. They are the father, the mother and the teacher. Let us join together and launch this movement from the home and the school to eradicate corruption.

## Conclusion

We are a large country, we are also blessed with natural resources and a highly motivated young human resources. We have to prioritise our thoughts on national development and make all other issues as, 'non-issues'. This will ensure focus and thrust for the development process. And it will prevent dissipation of energy and resources on non-productive issues.

All of us rare to place a moratorium on all issues which are impediments to the development of the nation, from now and pledge ourselves to make the missions of developed India a reality.

□

---

*On the eve of the 57th Independence Day on 14-08-2003.*

# 7
# Indomitable Spirit

It is very important to recognize outstanding employees, employers, placement officers, individuals, institutions and creative disabled persons from different walks of life. Government institutions should respect the disability Bill which provides three percent job reservations for disabled persons. There must be a mechanism for effective monitoring of adherence to the Bill by the concerned ministries and departments, so that the disabled personnel are able to lead an economically independent normal life. Just like Government departments it is also essential that industries and service sectors to consider good human services in employing disabled persons.

## Disabled Population as the Mission

It is estimated that in India the disabled persons constitute 5% of the total population. I would request the Ministry of Social Justice and Empowerment to work out the statistics within a year. The holistic rehabilitation of these persons involves a multisectoral approach and creation of a condition in which they can fully realize their potential and live their lives as independently and work and contribute. Presently it is estimated that less than 20% of the disabled population alone are brought under the purview of rehabilitation schemes. Majority of the disabled who are not receiving any rehabilitation aid or advice belong to the rural sector and they remain only under parental care and suffer the pain all through their lives. It is necessary to have counselling for the parents and relatives of the disabled and motivate them to come forward to seek the help of specialist agencies who can assist them in getting the right supportive devices and general/vocational training for their wards. In addition to providing vocational training, it is essential for government and non-governmental agencies to give psychological training for 3 to 6 months to create a spirit of "We can do it, we will win," among the disabled persons. Combination of vocational training and the higher efforts of the disabled persons will generate the indomitable spirit. I would like to share with you some of my thoughts on this crucial human welfare mission of "Indomitable spirit."

**Indomitable Spirit**

The perception of disability lies in the mind. Surely a person with a pure and enlightened mind is a valuable citizen irrespective of whether he is physically disabled or not. The life of a disabled person can be enriched through creation of indomitable spirit in them. I would like to share one example of an individual who have excelled in his field with all the disabilities.

During my visit to Bulgaria I visited National Art Gallery. There I saw an exhibition of paintings, mostly done by Bulgarian painters which inspired and impressed me. I also saw 100th birth anniversary exposition of the famous Bulgarian artist Zlatju Bojadjiev. Hundreds of paintings were done by him using right hand as is normally done. I was told that his right hand subsequently was paralyzed. But the indomitable spirit in him, made him paint using his left hand and these more beautiful paintings were also displayed. That struck me, that constructive people cannot be hampered by a physical defect, as the power comes from inside to make one to go ahead with the mission of his life.

I would like to suggest few societal and technological support missions needed for making disabled persons to live near normal life.

### Disability Friendly Education and Working Place

One of the important concerns is to provide easy accessibility to public buildings, schools, colleges, banks, transport etc. I understand Delhi Metro Rail Corporation has made proper provisions for the benefit of those who are physically challenged. We should make all efforts to provide conducive working environment with easy accessibility. A tripartite approach to handle, educate and empower the disabled has to be in place with the assistance of parents, teachers and social service/health care agencies. Technological and industrial partners in this effort should aim at providing affordable devices and dependable services.

We have to make efforts to ensure that disabled persons get equal opportunities and they do not remain isolated in the society. We have to provide "equalization of opportunity," for persons with disabilities by providing seemingly simple, basic, and obvious services as access ramps and sidewalk indentations for the convenience of the disabled people. We need to realize the fact that this society is for all, encompassing human diversity and leading to development of the human potential in each person.

Assertive devices can often minimize handicaps. While we have developed many new and useful items, we need to pay attention to quality as well as at affordable cost. Research and development in this field is vital. We must harness Information Technology to improve access to the printed word for persons with visual impairment. While text in English can be scanned, transferred to the computer and heard through voice software, this facility is not yet available for the Indian languages at the speed and sophistication of English language. While material in English can easily be transcribed into Braille, this facility is not available for many of the Indian languages. Consequently, availability of text books and other reading materials in the Indian languages in Braille is scarce and production is expensive and time-consuming. I suggest the IT community to device a Braille keyboard with the necessary software to convert the Braille input into text and speech in the Indian languages.

## Technology for Disabled

When I was in Kolkata interacting with 9000 children at the Netaji Indoor Stadium, one boy suffering from visual impairment asked me, "Sir, what kind of education facilities are provided in the Knowledge Society, for visually handicapped children like me?" There are many like him. Let me share one thought with you. I had met many physically and mentally challenged children, visiting Rashtrapati Bhavan and also during my visits to various States and different countries. My belief all along was reconfirmed that these children like all others have an equal urge to pursue their studies and work. We have to provide solutions to their problems with the aid of Information Technology, by developing audio books, talking websites, voice assistive interfaces and other devices. We should launch programmes with IT institutions for developing aids for the visually handicapped at an affordable cost.

## Internet and Disabled

I visualize a scene in which some of the disabled have to become part of the Internet culture. Lack of access to the right information at the right time is a bothering concern for the disabled. Information and Communication Technology (ICT) will provide solution to make Internet friendly towards differently challenged individuals enabling them to benefit from the awesome power of the Internet. Physical mobility of the disabled may be minimised or eliminated by the virtual office concepts in which people are allowed to work from their homes through computers and deliver their work output to their offices online.

Even while we work towards such near-futuristic possibilities, we should also try to provide existing services for the disabled. For example, why not provide mobile telephones at a lower cost to those who are disabled as they need it the most for regular work and his/her safety?

## Indigenous Manufacturing of Critical Support Systems

Another area of concern is in India, we do not have Cochlear Implant manufacturing units. Cochlear implant helps the deaf and dumb individuals to regain near normal hearing/speaking capabilities. Basically it is by-passing the damaged inner ear portion by replacing its functions with an electronic system having external mike, speech processing circuit, transmitter and an receiver. The receiver is implanted below the ear. The receiver has an electrode which will be inserted into the cochlear portion of the ear. Speech processor processes the input audio signals and converts them into electrical signals in various channels. The transmitter transmits these signals to the implant's multi-channel electrode which terminates in various points of the cochlear. At a Hospital in Coimbatore, I saw children who could hear and converse after implanting and subsequent IT-aided training. The cost of imported cochlear implant is around Rupees 7 lakhs which common man cannot afford. Series of development activities should be initiated to establish cochlear implant manufacturing capabilities in India with the objective of bringing down the cost of all components, surgery and post-operative training to around Rupees 40 to 50 thousand.

## Mentally Challenged Children Research

At Anna University, I was also guiding a doctoral research project. The research is to find a software/

hardware integrated solution to achieve a near normal functioning of the brain of mentally challenged children. When I saw some of the mentally challenged children performing certain activities like singing, painting in Central Institute of Mentally Retardation, Thiruvananthapuram, I was convinced that one day convergence of information and communication technology, medical electronics, biotechnology and mathematical simulation can find a solution for their problem. We have been studying the mentally challenged children in various research institutions, homes for mentally retarded and hospitals. We were sure that by transforming the functions of the damaged portion of the brain to the normal portion of the brain by some triggering mechanism, or by implanting a bio chip to carry out those functions, the retardation process can be arrested and rejuvenation of the damaged cells can take place. The problem is very complex. Can it be solved? The research still continues.

## Women with Disabilities

In every sphere of life, women with disabilities are very high. The unemployment rate for disabled women is phenomenally high. Government and social organisations, educational institutions and industry have to work together and evolve methods for removing the high rate of unemployment of women having disability and bring them into main-stream of life by building capacity in them to make useful contribution to nation building tasks.

## Rehabilitation

Rehabilitation process should aim at enabling persons with disabilities to reach and maintain their optimal physical, sensory, intellectual, psychological and/or social functional levels, thus providing them with the tools to change their lives towards a higher level of independence. Rehabilitation process has to include measures to provide and/or restore functions, or compensate for the loss or absence of a function or for a functional limitation. It should include a wide range of measures and activities from more basic and general rehabilitation to goal-oriented activities, for instance vocational rehabilitation.

The most important need is to enlist people as support group personnel who have love and passion for serving others. Advanced composite technologies are helping the disabled to have light weight artificial limbs or FROs (Floor Reaction Orthosis) – Calipers. I could see the happiness of the recipients in Bhuj after earthquake disaster. Composite material may also used for making Braille. These types of technologies should be adopted on a large-scale. There is a need to launch projects in these areas immediately.

## Conclusion

We require an innovative and caring mind to provide productive employment to the disabled persons. To achieve this, a committee of experts including representatives from corporate and voluntary sectors has identified around 120 occupations at executive/management/supervisory levels and around 946 occupations at skilled/semi-skilled/unskilled levels for employing disabled persons without compromising the quality of work. Organisations and industry should voluntarily come forward to offer some of the occupations to the disabled so that they can realize their economic independence and also have the satisfaction of contributing to the cause of removing pain. Now the call centres are becoming important business centres in the country. With the minimum hardware changes through a short training programme the call centres can employ large number of visually handicapped persons for efficient work in their establishments. I would recommend call centre institutions all over the country to facilitate conduct of such courses for the disabled persons in mission mode and provide employment.

Ministry of Social Justice and Empowerment should provide such support and encouragement necessary to promote the welfare of disabled persons to make them feel more secure, independent and be equal partners in the community.

Here I reproduce a poem written by Mustafa, a handicapped child in Persian language:

**Courage**

I don't have legs.
My mind says: Don't weep, don't weep
For, I need not bow even in front of a King.

□

---

*Address at National Award for the Welfare of Persons with Disabilities, New Delhi on 03-12-2003.*

# 8

# Education, Learning and Creativity

## Technology Dimensions

Technology has multiple dimensions. One leads to economic prosperity and the other creates the capability for national security. For the past 40 years, one-way or other I have witnessed these multi dimensions of technology. For example, the developments in chemical engineering brought fertilizers for higher yield of crops while the same science led to chemical weapons. Likewise, rocket technology developed for atmospheric research led to the launching satellites for remote sensing and communication applications which are vital for the economic development. The same technology led to the development of missiles with specific defence needs that provides said security for the nation. The aviation technology development has led to fighter and bomber aircraft, and the same technology assisted in designing a passenger jet and also help operations requiring quick reach of support to people affected by disasters. When nuclear science was born in 1940s, within two decades multiple applications like nuclear medicine, nuclear irradiation for preservation of agricultural products, nuclear power and later nuclear science led to weapons development and even deployment.

Computer science and mathematical science coupled with communication technology led the world to information technology. Using Information Technology, various fields of administration, commerce, health and education have transformed into e-governance, e-commerce, telemedicine, and teleeducation. One phenomenon which we have witnessed, particularly in India with demand for software development because of national and international requirement, the availability of elementary school, primary and secondary school teachers who love teaching reduced for the reasons that there were many opportunities in the other fields.

## Two-Way Teaching and Learning

The number of teachers, who love teaching as a Guru level, has to increase in large numbers. In view of the various demand pattern, shortage in this area may also be increasing. One side we saw prospective fields including Information Technology absorbing prospective good teachers. But now we have an opportunity to use same Information Technology with Communication Technology for entering into the era of teleeducation by creating network of multiple classrooms located in various schools built on the quality teachers bi-directional teaching and learning in the national level.

The model I envisage is the following: Every state can identify x thousand number of excellent teachers of primary and secondary schools. Using these teachers as resource in teleeducation using connectivity, with proper software and with bandwidth, the student strength can be increased from a normal strength of 40-60 students to more than 1000 students with multiple classroom. Increased use of e-education will bring down the cost of operations. Simultaneously rural connectivity (physical, electronic, knowledge and economic), will assist quality teachers preferring teaching in rural schools.

## Computers and Teaching

Every one of us have gone through the various phases

of education from the childhood to profession. A scene appears in front of me where there is a child, a teenager, an adult and a leader. Let me narrate to you how each one reacts to one particular situation? The situation is: human need. The child asks, "What can you do for me"? The teenager says, "I want to do it alone." The young person proclaims, "Let us do it together." The leader offers, "What can I do for you." So, the educational system have got a tremendous responsibility to transform a child into a leader – the transformation of, 'what can you do for me', to, 'what I can do for you'. That will demand a principal to be a visionary with an inspiring capability. Also the principals and teachers have to impart learning to the children in such a way to bring out the best in them, for this he or she has to be a good teacher himself. With the trends of recent reform efforts in mind, how does technology fit into the scheme of revolutionizing education? Computers provide ample assistance in accomplishing numerous reform goals. In terms of actual instruction, computers are an invaluable tool for providing active collaborative learning and assessment. While basic word-processing programs allow students to become independent publishers of ideas and opinions, e-mail provides opportunities for peer review and group editing.

More sophisticated interactive multimedia packages offer true inquiry-based learning, where students must construct and demonstrate solutions to a variety of in-class projects. This is not to suggest that computers are used in reform to replace the role of the teacher; realistically that would be both undesirable and impractical. Instead, the computer must be recognised as an effective teaching tool which assists the educator. Software offer students individualised learning, so while some students progress on a subject at their own paces, those who begin to fall behind can receive proper interpersonal attention from the instructor. The computer assists the teacher to concentrate on interaction and individualised assistance.

## Prime Learning: Education with Value

The best part of a young person is his or her childhood in school and the best time spent is 0800 Hrs to 1600 Hrs in the school. The prime learning environment is 5th to 16th years of age. The student spends approximately 20,000 hours in the school campus. Of course, at home, love and affection are imparted but again most of the time of the day is spent in preparing school's homework and study, eat, play and sleep. Hence the school hours for children are the best time for learning and need best of environment, mission-oriented learning with value system. I still hear the echo from Bestolozzy, a great teacher's saying, "Give me a child for seven years. Afterwards, let the God or devil take the child. They cannot change the child." For parents and teachers, school campus and home have to have an integrated mission: education with value system. Children have to be given value-based education in the school so that government or society can establish a transparent society or a society with integrity. Principals and teachers are the Gurus, the role model, the Gurus can instill creativity. Computer becomes user friendly tool. The vision is indeed bigger than who have assembled here.

## The Teacher puts You, Decades Ahead

Another incident was at St. Joseph's College, Tiruchirapalli. As a young student, we had the opportunity at St. Joseph's College witnessing a scene, a unique, divine looking personality walking through the college campus every morning teaching Mathematics BSc (Honours) and MA (Mathematics) students. Young students looked with awe and respect, a personality symbolizing our own culture. When he walked, knowledge radiated all around. The great personality was, Prof. T. Totadri Iyengar, the great teacher. At that time, 'Calculus Srinivasan', was my mathematics teacher. Calculus Srinivasan used to talk about Prof. Totadri Iyengar with deep respect. During those days, he and Prof. Totadri Iyengar had an understanding to have an integrated class by Prof. Totadri Iyengar for first year B.Sc. (Hons) and first year B.Sc. (Physics). I had the opportunity to attend his classes, particularly on the subjects of modern algebra, statistics and also once I heard him teaching complex variables. When we were in the BSc first year, Calculus Srinivasan used to select top ten students to the Mathematics Club of St. Joseph's to where Prof. Totadri Iyengar used to give lecture series. One day, in 1952, I still remember, he gave a one hour lecture on ancient mathematicians and astronomers of India and introduced four great mathematician and astronomers. For nearly one hour he spoke. The lecture is still ringing in my ears. I was introduced to the pride of the nation: pioneers in astronomy and mathematics (4th to 20th century), Aryabhata, Bhaskara and Ramanujam who gave to the world, the value of zero to number, orbit period of earth around sun and recently number theory. The two incident narrated have become the foundation for my education, learning with hope and value system. My teachers of primary, secondary and college education had put me few decades ahead. This is indeed the vision. Today's young dream transforming India into a knowledge society. I am sure the younger generation, with the amount of inputs and exposure they gain using various information technology tools, will be able to understand the technological developments and prepare themselves with competencies and courage to face the global competitive environment.

## Knowledge Society and Education

A task team of Planning Commission has worked on the study on how India can be transformed into a knowledge society in a decade. India is a nation endowed with natural and competitive advantages as also certain distinctive competencies. But these are scattered in isolated pockets and the awareness on these is inadequate. During the last century the world has undergone a change from agriculture society, where natural labour was the critical factor, to industrial society where the management of technology, capital and labour provided the competitive advantage. In the 21st century, a new society is emerging where knowledge is the primary production resource instead of capital and labour. Efficient utilisation of this existing knowledge can create comprehensive wealth of the nation in the form of better health, education, infrastructure and other social indicators.

Such a knowledge society has two very important components driven by societal transformation and wealth generation. The societal transformation is on education, healthcare, agriculture and governance. These will lead to employment generation, high productivity and rural prosperity. How do we do that?

The wealth generation is a very important task for the nation, which has to be woven around national competencies. The task team has identified core areas that will spearhead our march towards knowledge society. The areas are: Information Technology, biotechnology, weather forecasting, disaster management, telemedicine and teleeducation, technologies to produce native knowledge products, service sector and Infotainment which is the emerging area resulting from convergence of information and entertainment. The driving force for a knowledge society is the primary and secondary education. There is shortage of competent teachers who love teaching. Computer literacy will facilitate teaching competency and increase the scope of student audience to every good programs. have a network of good schools.

One solution is to adopt distance education as a means of bringing education to every eligible child, together with innovative schemes and incentives to attract all children to attend the school. One full satellite transponder gives adequate bandwidth to provide a full range of curriculum from pre-school and nursery to the 12th standard. Technology based learning has to become an important curriculum in schools.

While classroom learning is important, what the child learns by self-observation outside the classroom is equally important. A child must become an active participant in the process of learning through observation, field studies, experiments and discussions. A child's individuality and creativity needs to be given due importance in our education. Further, in addition to innovation in curriculum, priority needs to be given to the reorientation of the outlook of the teachers and more effective examination system so that it recognises and evaluates creativity and new thinking. The schools must move from becoming educational centers to knowledge and skill centers. I am sure that computers and vast information source available on the internet can assist the teachers and hence the schools.

## Conclusion

There is a national mission for universal primary education. Good teachers and parents select the schools for high academic standards, focus on teaching and learning, education philosophy with value system close to their own and above all innovative approaches in instruction. Of course, schools are sought where students are challenged to achieve higher levels.

In conclusion, the schools have a great mission to ignite the minds of the young. The ignited minds of the young are the most powerful resource on the earth, above the earth and under the earth. Thinking is progress. Our schools have to lead the education in which the creativity of the children blossom and the nation prospers.

□

---

*Presenting the 1st Computer Literacy Excellence Awards for Schools-2002, New Delhi on 29-08-2002.*

# 9
# Marvels of the Universe

Vikrant Nahal Arya of Sanskriti School and Rupanjali Lahiri of St Thomas School, New Delhi asked me very simple question which led me to think. The question was: "Your birthday has recently gone by. What were your thoughts on that day?" They wanted to know what my birthday meant to me. It meant for me that I had completed 71 orbits around the sun, and had entered my 72nd orbit. Think of our Universe. I am amazed and always inspired by the dynamics of our universe. Our star (sun), its planets, every celestial object has a purpose. If the Earth stopped rotating around its axis, what would happen? No earth, No night, No day. If Sun does not orbit, sun will not be there. Think of it. The sun also orbit around the Milky Way. Isn't it. It takes the Sun 250 million years for one orbit around Milky Way, our galaxy. Compare that to my 72nd orbits. What does that mean? One single citizen completing 71 orbits. It is an insignificant event, compared to dynamics of universe. But human mind is innovative and can think and explore the marvels of universe.

## Thinking is Progress

We should note that human mind is a unique gift. Marvels of universe you can enter into it only if you have curiosity and thinking. I suggest to all of you, thinking should become your capital asset, no matter whatever ups and downs you come across in your life. Thinking is progress. Non-thinking is destruction to the individual, organization and the country. Thinking leads to action. Knowledge without action is useless and irrelevant. Knowledge with action brings prosperity.

As a student, you should have a mind to explore every aspect of human life. Look at the sky. We are not alone. The whole universe is friendly to us and conspires to give the best to those who dream. Like Chandrasekhar Subramaniam discovered the black hole. Today, using Chandrasekar's limit we can calculate how long the sun will shine. Like, Sir C.V. Raman looked at the sea and questioned why the sea should be blue leading to the birth of Raman Effect. Like, Albert Einstein, armed with the complexity of the universe, asked the question how the universe was born. The famous equation $E = mc^2$ arrived. When $E = mc^2$ is in the hands of noble souls we got electricity using nuclear materials. When the same equation was in the hands of extreme political thinkers, destruction of Hiroshima took place. Millions of people walk in this universe. But during last millennium one noble soul walked and walked in the Indian soil giving application of *ahimsa, dharma* leading to the Indian independence. My dear friends, can you dream to become a noble minded like Mahatma Gandhi or Sir C.V. Raman or Einstein, or Chandrasekhar Subramaniam. Look at the marvels of your universe. You become a great thinker and action will follow.

### Knowledge Sweat and Perseverance

Everywhere, one common voice echoed from the young. Mr. Kalam, can you tell us, in this complex world how to achieve a prosperous India, peaceful India, a secured India? What can be my answer? I was thinking and thinking. I have lived in this planet for 71 years. Did I learn out of my difficult times, some thing to share with you, the young boys and girls across the country. From 1982 to 1992 was a very important period for me to design, develop, build and to operate certain missile systems for our country. What type of world was there around me at that time. All developed countries had condemned India in the name of MTCR, as one weapon. The other weapon used by them was NPT (Non nuclear Proliferation Treaty). With these two weapons of technological denials can the Indian minds succeed in its mission? I will share with you an experience which I had during development of Prithvi and Agni missile systems. In the missile system, for guidance and control, we use two gyro sensors in every flight system. For a given accuracy for a missile payload system, it was essential to have a accuracy of .20 drift per hour. One of our industries at that time was producing 10 per hour gyros. There was a denial of high accuracy gyros from developed countries. A task team was formed between an University and one of our labs to find a technical solution. About twelve software and hardware engineers after working for eight months came out with a solution of fast algorithm to be loaded on the on-board computer of the missile system and for real time error compensation. This will predict the error in the flight trajectory ahead and compensate the error in the gyro performance to make it to provide very high accuracy than the one which was denied. Here is an example how software solutions, knowledge and enthusiasm can work with hardware constraints. We have to work for high end software which will bring more value addition. Also, VLSI foundries should be continuously upgraded to the sub-micron level. To keep these foundries going, one of the major requirement is high purity VLSI grade silicon material. The country should have this facility and the investment should take place in this critical area.

### The Vision for the Nation

India should become a developed country. This is the

second vision for the nation. How we can prepare ourselves to this challenge?

To become a developed India, the essential needs are (a) India has to be economically and commercially powerful, at least to be one of the four top nations in terms of size of the economy. Our target should be a GDP growth of 9% annually and that the people below poverty line to be reduced to 10%. (b) Near self-reliance in defence needs of weapon, equipment with no umbilical attached to any outside world. (c) India should have a right place in world forums. Technology Vision 2020 is a pathway to realise this cherished mission.

### Technology Vision 2020

The Technology Vision 2020 consisted of 17 technology packages in the core sectors such as agriculture and food, healthcare, infrastructure and strategic industries. The Task Teams with nearly 500 experts of our country worked for two years, deliberated national status of various branches of national development and generated 35 documents detailing the steps to be taken for creating wealth for the nation and the well-being of our people. 'Technology', is the most vital key for achieving the goals. The vision deals with agrofood processing, food and agriculture, healthcare, electric power, civil aviation, waterways, engineering industries, life sciences and biotechnology, strategic industries and materials and processing. There is a tremendous link between each technology package. For example, higher food production and productivity which is essential, can be achieved, by incorporating technological excellence in scientific inputs for cultivation, harvesting, storage as well as transportation, distribution, marketing, preservation of seeds, improved pesticides, etc.

We have identified five areas where India has a core competence for an integrated action. (1) Agriculture and food processing – we have to put a target of 360 million tons of food and agricultural production. Other areas of agriculture and agrofood processing would bring prosperity to rural people and speed up the economic growth. (2) Reliable and quality electric power for all parts of the country. (3) Education and Healthcare – we have seen, based on the experience, education and healthcare are interrelated. For example, Kerala with education and better healthcare can bring down the population growth and provide improvements in quality of life of the people. Similarly, in Tamil Nadu also we have seen the downward growth of population resulting from a unique system of 'mid-day meal', coupled with education. Studies about Andhra Pradesh also have different facets. These experiences, we feel, should be taken and spread in big states like Bihar and Uttar Pradesh. Beginning of agricultural prosperity through better yields in these States will help this process. (4) Information Technology – This is one of our core competence. We believe, this area can be used to promote education in remote areas and also to create national wealth. (5) Strategic sectors – This area, fortunately, witnessed the growth in nuclear technology, space technology and defence technology. Other areas like Advanced Sensors and Materials would need a push. The nation has a plan towards 70% near self-reliance in a decade in defence equipment.

These five areas are closely interrelated and lead to national, food, and economic security. A strong partnership among the R&D, academy, industry and the community as a whole with the Government departments will be essential to accomplish the vision.

The vision for a developed India is even though driven fully by economic development coupled with security needs of the nation, it is important to note that the intellectuals of the nation is equally important. What it means is: India, due to its ancient civilisation, inspite of overpowering from various invading nations, the intellectual wisdom needs to be sprung back, matched with Indian value system. The intellectuals' mighty minds built in self-confidence with compassion for the service to poorer section is the most important demand for a developed nation – happy society.

## Conclusion

The present academic system may give you more workload, But, it doesn't prevent you to dream. It doesn't prevent you to work hard and acquire knowledge. Hard work and perseverance are beautiful angels who will support you. I would like to recall an incident that I witnessed in 1960s. Prof. Vikram Sarabhai, the visionary of space programme, put forth to this country that India should design and develop communication satellites, remote sensing satellites and launch them in polar orbits from the Indian soil, for mapping Indian natural resources. Today his dream has become true. The nation is capable of developing any type of space system. Hence, dream. Your dreams will transform into thoughts. The thoughts will result in actions and it will turned into success.

India is a nation of a billion people. A nation's progress depends upon how its people think. It is thoughts which are transformed into actions. India has to think as a nation of a billion people. I am sure, the recommendations of this Summit will facilitate proper actions. Let the young minds blossomfull of thought, the thoughts of prosperity.

□

---

*Inaugural Address at the First Child Education Summit-2002, New Delhi on 14-11-2002.*

# 10
# Knowledge Empowered with Creativity

In the vision for developed India, rural development is one of the important requirements. And, handicrafts play a major role for rural development because India has the core competence in handicrafts in her villages in the mountains, deserts and coastal regions. I come from Rameswaram island. I remember, it was in 1940s, the palm leaf baskets were made in many houses for their earning. This activity was supposed to be an additional unstructured small-scale business. Each day, a trader used to pay and collect all the finished products from these craftspeople. Even in Pulicat, near Chennai, craftswork is predominantly done. Also, during my young days at Rameswaram, I have seen, many houses were involved in sea shells craftswork. They used to get these shells from the sea, clean it with acid and do etching. These come out in beautiful shapes and wonderful art work. The craftswork and handicrafts, what I have seen in Ramanathapuram district and many other parts of our country should be nurtured with value addition.

During my visit I found, every State has a unique craftsmanship, but the income is not proportionate to the effort and time of each craftsman in making the handicrafts products. Time has come to view that craftsmanship is made a part of the economy through mission mode operation. During my recent visits to five North-Eastern States,

I observed one in every fourteen of the population depends on handicrafts. These products can be clothing, hardware, tools or even headgear for various applications for their daily use. They not only speak of the culture and beauty, but also reveal that the people depend on handicrafts for their earning. It is, therefore, all the more important to solve problems associated with marketing handicrafts products with value addition through craftsman-friendly technologies integrating multiple departments in a mission mode. This will facilitate exploiting export market from the present ₹ 6000 Crores to ₹ 60,000 Crores per year in the next 5 years.

## Knowledge Powered Rural Complex

The work of craftspeople and artisans is the result of creativity. This creativity comes from traditional knowledge. The crafts products from this traditional knowledge are of constant attack from urban industrial and multinational products (e.g. palm leaf, coir and rubber products versus plastic products). The traditional knowledge is in isolation in rural environment. This traditional knowledge has to be integrated with technology with value addition and proactive cooperative societies to empower craftspeople and artisans, making avenues for direct marketing/ selling. Instead of craftspeople coming to urban marketing centres, the reverse phenomena have to take place. How is it possible? Knowledge powered village complex has to be generated in numbers in every State. That means, 20-30 villages linked through a circular road (10 × 6 kms) with highways connectivity and electronically connected and also continuous functional transport system. In the periphery, there can be schools, primary health centres, craftspeople working and training centres, silos for storage of products and markets for promoting products of craftspeople and cottage industries. This knowledge powered village complex will also have markets attracting urban business.

The Regional Design and Technical Development Centres located in the cities need to move to rural areas. Mobile technology feeders for craftsmanship, support of design tools like CAD and Virtual Reality will further add value to the products to attract international market.

I have read, 'Inner Recesses Outer Spaces', by Kamaladevi Chattopadhyay, 'Visvakarma's Children' by Jaya Jaitley and 'Indian Sculpture and Iconography', by Dr. Ganapati Sthapathi. There may be many more books by the creators of art. When I read all these books, a thought came to my mind. These creators of arts must have a mission to spread their knowledge to thousands of artists as a profession and business opportunity.

## Conclusion

I am sure the initiatives taken by the Ministry of Textiles to empower craftspersons through inputs on design and technology and partnership with the NGOs and entrepreneurs will ensure sustainable development in this sector leading to a good share in the Indian economy. They will transmit their skill to many artists so that excellence continues to be the hallmark of our crafts.

□

*Inaugural Address at the Golden Jubilee Celebrations of Handicrafts Resurgence in India, New Delhi on 15-11-2002.*

# 11

# The Scientist Who Inspire United States

Have you heard about Thumba? It is in Kerala on the seashore. This is the place from where Indian space program commenced. It is a big story how Thumba was selected for space program. Prof. Vikram Sarabhai, a Cosmic rays Scientist and Homi Bhabha a Nuclear Scientist were searching for a place from where they can launch sounding rockets for atmospheric research, ionospheric research and meteorological research. After seeing various places, they came to a conclusion that Thumba is the right place as it is very close to the Equator which will help the space research in equatorial zones. That's how NIKE CAGUN – a two staged rocket was launched in Nov 1963. That was a Indo-US Cooperation Program. Within six years time, Prof. Vikram Sarabhai unfurled the space mission for India that should build Satellite Launch Vehicle capability, to put communication satellite in the geosynchronous orbit and remote sensing satellite in the polar orbit. Also, he envisaged that launch vehicles built in India should be launched from Indian soil. This one visionary thought led to intensive research in multiple fields of science and space technology. Today, India with her 20,000 scientific technological and support staff in multiple space research centres have the capability to build any type of satellite launch vehicles, any type of rockets and launch it from Indian soil. I had the fortune to be part of Prof. Vikram Sarabhai's vision and my team and myself to participate in India's first satellite launch vehicle programme to put the satellite in the orbit. Friends, can you please tell, what did you understand from this experience.

Millions of people walk in this universe. But during last millennium one noble soul walked and walked in the Indian soil giving application of *ahimsa, dharma* leading to the Indian independence. Freedom for India resulted in 1947 on a single question "India needs freedom." In 1950s there was a tremendous shortage for food. We had to depend on wheat ships that come crossing Atlantic ocean to prevent famine in India. The political leader C. Subramaniyam and an agricultural scientist Mr. M.S. Swaminathan asked a question in 1950s. How long India can depend on the imported food from developed countries? Let us become self-sufficient in food. That thought led to green revolution resulting from technology, agricultural science and farmers participation. Similar thoughts when came to Mr. Verghese Kurien, the milk man of India, India could attain surplus Milk Production. We produce Milk and Milk products in excess of our requirement. What is science? Science is asking series of questions and finding the right answer through hard work resulted into laws of nature or technological advancements. So children, who are attending the science congress, one of the suggestion I can give you Don't get afraid of asking questions. Go on asking till you get satisfied answer. Only questioning minds have made the world to live livable in spite of world's non-linear dynamics.

## Knowledge, Sweat and Perseverance

The best part for a person is his or her learning period in school childhood. The prime learning environment is 5th to 16th years' of age. Of course at home, love and affection are imparted. But again most of the time in a day is spent in preparing school's homework and study, eat, play and sleep. Hence the school hours for children are the best time for learning and need the best of environment and mission-oriented learning with value system. During this stage, they need value based education in school and at home for them to become good citizens. This reminds me the echo from Bestolozzy, a great teacher's saying, "Give me a child for seven years. Afterwards, let the God or devil take the child. They cannot change the child." For parents and teachers, school campus and home have to have an integrated mission: education with value system. If the child misses the value-based education of 25,000 hours in the school campus, no government or society can establish a transparent society or a society with integrity. Up to the age of 17 years, the father, the mother and the teacher lead a child to become an enlightened citizen. I also consider learning is a continuous process and knowledge acquisition continues.

Now I would like to explain the result of the hard work and perseverance with one of my experience. It was in conjunction with Prof. Sarabhai's vision for space programmes. Design project of India's first satellite launch vehicle was approved. Design of each stage of rocket, heat shield, guidance system was given to selected project leaders. I was given the 4th stage of SLV-3, that is upper stage rocket to give final velocity to put Rohini into orbit. The 4th stage SLV, uses an apogee motor, it should give the maximum thrust with minimum weight condition. It has critical technology. Hence, it was made out of composite structures which gives light weight. It is in early 1969 I remember, I received a call from Prof. Sarabhai from Ahmedabad stating that he will be visiting Trivandrum along with Prof. Curien, President of a French Space Organisation. I was asked to give a presentation about the 4th stage to Prof. Curien's team. When the presentation by my team was over, we realised that SLV-3 4th stage is also being considered for a French 4th stage launch vehicle 'Diamont' P-4 and French Organisation was looking for an apogee rocket motor nearly double the propellant weight and also size of the stage what we had designed. A decision was taken in the same meeting that SLV's fourth stage should be reconfigured to match and suit both French satellite launch vehicles and Indian launch vehicles. I would like to give the picture of the status at that time of our rocket technology. It was in the drawing board and of design status. Here is a visionary whose dream that Indian scientists will build an upper stage rocket system compatible both for Indian and French satellite launch vehicle system. What a confidence he put on the Indian scientific community?

A decision was taken that this upper stage has to be designed and developed and it was projectised. This event was remarkable and motivating for us. We went on full swing. A series of reviews took place between the two teams. The 4th stage graduated from drawing board to developing stage. Then in 1971 Prof. Sarabhai passed away at the same time the Diamont P-4 programme was called off and to be reconfigured in future. When the 4th stage was developed and series of tests were going on, a new requirement appeared in the horizon that is India building small communication satellites to be integrated as one of the piggyback satellite in the Ariane programmes (European Space Launch Programme). For our Indian Apple programme that is communication satellite – the SLV-3 4th stage exactly fitted and we flew in 1980s integrated in the European space launch from French Guiana Kourou. The vision seeded in 1969 by Prof. Vikhram Sarabhai was indeed realised when the apple satellite started transmitting a communication to Indian earth stations. This gives some insight of a visionary with committed scientific and support, we can realise the vision. Even we can built our rockets, can be flown in foreign soil. This achievement triggered rocket technologists in the country and it is indeed is the result of hard work and perseverance of the entire team. So dear friends, carry on you shoulder the angels and they are hard work, sweat and perseverance.

## The Vision for the Nation

To be developed nation is the second vision for the nation. When you are just entering into your life after education, you will enter into the theatre of action.

To become a developed India, the essential needs are (a) India has to be economically and commercially powerful, at least to be one of the four top nations in terms of size of the economy. Our target should be a GDP growth of 9% annually and that the people below poverty line to be reduced to 10%. (b) Near self-reliance in defence needs of weapon, equipment with no umbilical attached to any outside world. (c) India should have a right place in world forums. Technology Vision 2020 is a pathway to realise this cherished mission.

We have identified five areas where India has a core competence for an integrated action. (1) Agriculture and food processing – we have to put a target of 360 million tons of food and agricultural production. Other areas of agriculture and agrofood processing would bring prosperity to rural people and speed up the economic growth. (2) Reliable and quality electric power for all parts of the country. (3) Education and Healthcare (4) Information Technology – This is one of our core competence. (5) Strategic sectors.

These five areas are closely interrelated and lead to national, food, and economic security. A strong partnership among the R&D, academy, industry and the community as a whole with the Government departments will be essential to accomplish the vision.

## Conclusion

India is a nation of a billion people. A nation's progress depends upon how its people think. It is thoughts which are transformed into actions. India has to think as a nation of a billion people. I am sure, your thoughts in this science congress will enrich the decision-making process. Let the young minds blossomfull of thought, the thoughts of prosperity. My greetings and best wishes to all the young innovators.

□

---

*Inaugural Address at the National Children's Science Congress-2002, Mysore on 27-12-2002.*

# 12
# Power of the Ignited Minds

## Thumba to Geosynchronous Orbit

Have you heard about Thumba? It is in Kerala on the seashore. This is the place from where Indian space program commenced. It is a big story how Thumba was selected for space program. Prof. Vikram Sarabhai, a Cosmic Ray Scientist and Homi Bhabha a Nuclear Scientist were searching for a place from where they can launch sounding rockets for atmospheric research, ionospheric research and meteorological research. After seeing various places, they came to a conclusion that Thumba is the right place as it is very close to the Equator which will help the space research in equatorial zones. That's how NIKE CAJUN – a two staged rocket was launched in Nov 1963. That was a Indo-US Cooperation Program. Within six years time, Prof. Vikram Sarabhai unfurled the space mission for India that should build Satellite Launch Vehicle capability, to put India's communication satellite in the geosynchronous orbit and remote sensing satellite in the polar orbit. Also, he envisaged that launch vehicles built in India should be launched from Indian soil. This one visionary thought led to intensive research in multiple fields of science and space technology. Today, India with her 25,000 scientific technological and support staff in multiple space research centres have the capability to build any type of satellite launch vehicles, any type of rockets and launch it from

Indian soil. I had the fortune to be part of Prof. Vikram Sarabhai's vision and my team and myself to participate in India's first satellite launch vehicle programme to put the satellite in the orbit.

## India's Technological Progress

India after its independence was determined to move ahead with planned policies for Science and Technology. Now, India is very near to self-sufficiency in food, making the ship to mouth existence of 1950s, an event of the past. Also improvements in the health sector, have eliminated few contagious diseases. There is a increase in life-expectancy. Small-scale industries provide high percentage of National GDP – a vast change in 1990s compared to 1950s. Today India can design, develop and launch world class geo-stationary and sun synchronous, remote sensing satellites.

The nuclear establishments have reached the capability of building nuclear power stations, nuclear medicine and nuclear irradiation of agricultural seeds for growth in agricultural production. Today India has become a Nuclear Weapon State. Defence Research had led to design, development and production of Main Battle Tanks, strategic missile systems, electronic warfare systems and various armours. Also we have seen growth in the Information Technology; the country is progressing in hardware and software export business of more than 10 billion dollars even though there are low ebbs in the last few years. India yet is a developing country. What Technology can do further?

Technology has multiple dimensions. Geopolitics convert the technology to a particular nation's policy. The same policy will lead to economic prosperity and capability for national security. For example, the developments in chemical engineering brought fertilizers for higher yield of crops while the same science led to chemical weapons. Likewise, rocket technology developed for atmospheric research helped in launching satellites for remote sensing and communication applications which are vital for the economic development. The same technology led to the development of missiles with specific defense needs that provides security for the nation. The aviation technology development has led to fighter and bomber aircraft, and the same technology will lead to passenger jet and also help operations requiring quick reach of support to people affected by disasters. At this stage, let us study global growth of technology and impact in human life.

## Knowledge Society

India is going to enter in another decades time into a knowledge society. What type of knowledge society it is going to be?

A knowledge society can be one of the foundations for realizing the vision for the nation: Developed India. Knowledge has always been the prime mover of prosperity and power. The acquisition of knowledge has therefore been the thrust area throughout the world and sharing the experience of knowledge is a unique culture of our country. India is a nation endowed with natural and competitive advantages as also certain distinctive competencies. But these are scattered in isolated pockets and the awareness on these is inadequate.

## Agenda for the Young in Developed India Mission

Developed India will become a reality. The Prime Minister, on Independence Day-2002, had announced that we will become a Developed India by 2020. The largest beneficiary of this dream when realised will be you, the young. Hence it is important that you contribute in its initial stages of realization and shape it to the best of your abilities within your academic and family confines. The biggest concern of the parents and the children in your age group is about the job prospects when you complete your education. Without worrying about minor variations in the subjects of your pursuit, your opportunities and future will be brighter if you excel in whatever subject you undertake to study. At the frontier there are no borders. The employment opportunities are many, when a person becomes very selective like Government jobs, then there is tremendous constraints comes. If you open up your thoughts for entrepreneurship, design, industry, direct participation in agriculture with innovative ideas, making IT products etc. Most important thing for future young generation is to make up its mind to contribute in all sectors. The tool can be knowledge and physical contribution. In student life inspite of various constraints you can uniquely contribute for national development.

## Student Centric Literacy Movement

One of the important indicators of a developed nation is the literacy level. Educating a nation of a billion people is not a small task. It requires the participation of all the stake holders starting from the young. Many of you are fortunate enough to attend good schools for a quality education. But many of your brothers and sisters are not that fortunate, particularly those from the villages near you. A good sign of a developed nation is that it is built on societies wherein 'people who have', to work hard to bridge the divide between them and, "those who have not." One way of doing this is for your school to adopt a village near you. When we look at the national target of increasing the literacy level from 57% to 75% by 2010, you must set the target for the village you adopted to be in tune with the national mission. Each one of you could visit the villages on holidays and contribute to removal of illiteracy of at least two persons and light the quest for knowledge in them. Work with consortium of industries, philanthropists, NGOs and ensure that this task is sustainable and its impact can be measurable and quantified.

The educational institutions have to gear-up to evolve a curriculum that is sensitive to the social and technological needs of the Developed India. Student activities towards such missions could be seamlessly integrated with the existing curriculum so that the future members of the knowledge society are fully developed in all aspects of societal transformation.

## Student Centric Eco-care Movement

The trees and vegetation around us are the best transformers of energy from the sun on a sustainable basis for our utilization. In the process they provide us the most efficient way of cleaning up our environment, shelter for all living species, a source of food and energy. They are often associated with serene environments that facilitate creative thoughts and actions. As you know dreaming, and dreams transforming into action are important constituents of developed India, friends what you can contribute. Without pain and tears, 200 million of you, if you plant five seedlings, you will add a billion trees, and mother India will give her smiles to you. On that day you will demonstrate to the world that what 200 millions children can do collectively and make us proud. The tree planting may be done in your house, school or in the village your school adopts. The school management or the NGOs should help this student centric eco-care movement on a sustainable basis. Few years from now every one us, Indians, must be a proud guardian of trees planted by the young. This dynamic movement will echo the children's concern for eco-friendly future.

A billion trees also require careful planning water which is already becoming a scare commodity in this country. While the efforts are being taken to make the mother earth (*Dharati Maa*) greener, the rainwater due to lack of proper planning gets wasted. By todays technology, it is possible to develop a small-scale water harvesting stations. For example your school can think of developing a water harvesting station with 10 CFT per student within your school complex or in the village adopted by your school. If you do that the inbuilt thoughts in you will bring a spirit to share the national resources. Rainwater harvesting will maintain water table level preventing environmental decay and making water available for agriculture and drinking.

## Power of the Ignited Minds

When you are haunted with cultural invasions through media and elsewhere, think of you as children of civilisational bliss. We withstood multiple invasions and many dynasties ruled us. Today, India is free from invasions and is independent. We cherish the family values and spiritual life. Many developed nations are dreaming for such a full life. Our philosophy is, "Give them and go on giving."

When you hear the exaggerated turbulence in our society, have courage to feel that we are the nation of a billion people with multiple religions and languages. We are the largest democracy of continuity in this planet. No other nation has this unique strength of our experience. Spread this beautiful message everywhere.

When you get the defeatist state of mind, you cheer, because you belong to this great nation. We are self-reliant in food production, we make our own communication satellites, and also we launch our own remote sensing satellites. When India became, 'Nuclear Weapon State' and when India became a missile power, developed nations launched on us economic and technological sanctions in 1998 till date. We withstood and combated with our agricultural, technological, industrial might and above all the courage of our people. Keep this spirit and multiply with your dynamic momentum.

When you look around the world, you get discouraged, to think that, you belong to one of the hundreds of developing nations and not belong to the so-called developed 'G-8'.

Think of the billion ignited Indian minds. This is the most powerful resource compared to any resource on the earth, above the earth and below the earth. Our sweat will transform developing India into a developed nation. That is the vision, **India Millennium Mission 2020** – a developed India. Also, remember the famous saying of a poet, "I work, God honours me."

## Conclusion

A nation is great, not because a few people are great, but because every one in the nation is great. I wish you all to excel in your studies and become Doctors, Engineers, Scientists, Entrepreneurs, Officers of armed forces, Teachers, Lawyers, Administrators, Political Leaders and above all the best human beings with traditional value system and societal care. The challenge in the mission of the developed India calls for an important, cohesive and focused efforts of the young. Just like our first vision of Independence created leaders, I am sure you all will rise to the occasion and become professional in multiple areas.

I have composed the Song of Youth.

□

*Address Students at Nethaji Indoor Stadium, Kolkata on 21-01-2003.*

# 13

# Science Advances with Intellectual Might

There are events in human history to defeat the man continuously driven by the natural forces and objection and non-acceptance of co-community. Still our humanity strives to succeed and to explore the new avenues for enriching the human life and for improving the standard of living. He had indomitable spirit to overcome all these hurdles. It is true to any scientific research, in the field of defense, in the field of nuclear science, in the field of bio-tech and in the field of space technology and in many more areas including the school life.

From the second century AD, we had Ptolemic theory, in which all the stars including the sun was assumed to be orbiting around the earth. Even now several assumptions of Ptolemic theory are referred for basic approximations. But during sixteenth century, Copernicus, first time, provided the theory that earth rotates around its own axis and it also orbits around the sun. He also said that the sun is also in an orbit in the galaxy. Later in the seventeenth century, Galileo carried out several scientific experiments on Copernicus' theories and declared to the world that the earth is orbiting. No one believed his statements. The entire religious missionaries turned against him. He had to sacrifice his life to prove that he was right.

Isaac Newton provided the gravitational theory between the planets, moon, stars and the earth. This Newton's' Theory, gave the foundation for flight science. After Newton, Einstein came with general theory of relativity which gave first time all the orbital systems including our stars and the sun are in synchronous motion with respect to space and time. Famous Einstein energy equation $E = mc^2$ emerged. First time, questions were asked. How are we born? Are we alone? Who created us? Then the scientific research started for discovering unified theory bringing together all theories of Copernicus, Galileo, Newton and Einstein and Stephen Hawking's string theory, to establish how earth is born, how our star is born, how long our star will shine.

## Science Beyond Boundaries

In 1935, Chandrasekhar limit was evolved and he discovered black hole – here for first time it was established how long the sun will shine – about 5 million years or more. It looks to me man cannot permanently stay in earth – for many resources – like mineral and energy he has to explore in other planets and star. Closest to us, possible human habitat is the mars. Moon may be a mineral resource and space industry center. So friends when you are all growing-up you are going to make earth liveable environmentally, economically – for which you have to explore as Columbus did as Livingstone did, Neil Armstrong did. Planets and moons have become man's destination for human progress.

## Aryabhata's Aryabhatiyam

Aryabhata was both an astronomer and mathematician, born in 476 AD in Kusumapura (now called Patna). He was known to represent a summary of all maths at that point of time. Just when he was only 23 years old, he wrote his book Aryabhatiyam in two parts. He covered important areas like arithmetic, algebra (first ever contributor), trigonometry and of course, astronomy. He gave formulas for the areas of a triangle and a circle and attempted to give the volumes of a sphere and a pyramid. He was the first to give an approximation to 'pi' as the ratio of a circle's circumference and diameter arriving at the value of 3.1416.

## Bhaskara

Bhaskaracharya, as he was known, was another unique intellectual of his time. He was born in 1114 AD at Vijjalbada, located either in Karnataka or Maharashtra. He wrote the famous Siddhanthasiromani in four chapters. He dealt in astronomy and algebra and is known to be the first recognised mathematician who evolved value to zero from the concept based on Aryabhata's discovery – the number.

Now I realise the great meaning of Albert Einstein's saying, "We owe a lot to the Indians who taught us how to count, without, which no worthwhile scientific discovery could have been made." The foundation for scientific discovery indeed originated from India.

## Ramanujan

Next comes to our mind the greatest of all geniuses every known and acknowledged, and who lived within our present memory, Srinivasa Ramanujan. He lived only for less than 33 years (1887-1920), had no practical formal education or means of living. Yet, his inexhaustible spirit and love for his subject made him contribute to treasure houses of mathematical research – some of which are still under serious study and engaging all-available world mathematicians' efforts to establish formal proofs. Ramanujan was a unique Indian genius who could melt the heart of the most hardened and outstanding Cambridge mathematician Hardy. In fact, it is not an exaggeration to say that it was Hardy who discovered Ramanujan for the world. One of the tributes to Ramanujan says that, 'Every Integer is a personal friend of Ramanujan, Professor Hardy rated various geniuses on a scale of 100 and while he could put most of them in the range of around 30 with rare exceptions reaching say 60, he suggested that only the value of 100 would fit Ramanujan. There can be no better tribute to either Ramanujan or to Indian Heritage. His works cover vast areas including Prime Numbers, Hypergeometric Series, Modular Functions, Elliptic Functions, Mock Theta Functions, even magic squares, apart from serious side works on geometry of ellipses, squaring the circle etc.

It is hoped that eminent teachers who teach and inspire the young students of mathematics will continue their unmatched and noble services in the years to come thus ensuring another saga of the march of the Indian Brilliance in the current and following millennia too. Prof. S. Chandrasekhar led the great Indian mathematics tradition in foreign soil. Of course mathematics is universal. Now the great original tradition will be further blossomed in present days by Prof. C.S. Seshadri, Prof. J.V. Narlikar, Prof. M.S. Narasimhan, Prof. S.R.S. Varadhan, Prof. M.S. Raghunathan, Prof. Narender Karmakar and Prof. Ashok Sen, among other distinguished mathematicians we have and will be having.

## Make the Impossible Possible

Human flight is nothing but creativity of human mind and it undergoes several struggles to achieve excellence by exploring the space. In 1890, a great well-known scientist Lord Kelvin, who was the President of Royal Society of London said, "Any thing heavier than air cannot fly, and cannot be flown." With in two decades Wright Brothers proved man can fly of course at heavy human cost. On the successful completion of Moon Mission in 1961, Farnbraun, a very famous rocket designer, who built Saturn-V, to launch the capsule with astronauts and made moon walk a reality, in 1975 said, "If I am authorised, I will remove the word impossible." Now let us take the story of the planet earth. During the recent Columbia's space mission, on January 29, 2002 at 3.39 p.m., the astronauts Mc Cool and Ramon said to the ground station, "We are in a vantage point in space, the world looks marvellous from up here, so peaceful, so wonderful and so fragile...." Friends, those seven astronauts are no more with us. They have given so much of scientific inputs to the humanity. Also they have given a very important message that the earth is fragile.

All the technological advancements we have today, are the outcome of scientific exploration of scientist of a few centuries. At no time, man was beaten by problems. He strives continuously to subjugate failures. Problems and failures are always in orbit. Also successes are in orbits in abundance. Indomitable spirit captures the success and subjugates the problems. Now from the earth dynamics, earth-moon-mars-sun galaxy dynamics let us come down to earth problem. How do we make India a prosperous – peaceful and secured nation?

## Vision for the Nation

We got freedom in 1947, that was the result of first vision for the nation. This vision created best of leaders in many fields like politics, philosophy, science, technology and industry. In many aspects of life, improvement in literacy, agricultural products, strategic areas, certain small and large-scale industries took place. Now more than fifty years have gone by and we are called as one of the hundreds of developing countries, in a distinct way a separation from G-8 countries. We have many challenges. Nearly 300 million people who are below the poverty line have to join the mainstream of a good life. Hundred per cent literacy, health for all, multiple industrial and agricultural productivity and lifestyle with value system has to emerge. Hence we need the second vision for the nation to become developed.

## Technology Vision 2020

A developed country, in my opinion, is one which has the capability and the capacity to comprehensively look at wealth generation and wealth protection and thereafter evolve integrated strategies, technologies and missions to meet these objectives. It is also a fact that technology is the established currency of geopolitical power and in the Indian context, technology has to be the driving force for economical development and national security. Recognizing this and with the help of two different streams of national experts, one by TIFAC, an autonomous body under the Department of Science and Technology and another by Department of Defence Research & Development, involving a few hundred man-years of combined efforts, two types of document emerged. These were Technology Vision 2020 in 17 volumes and Integrated Strategies, Technologies and Missions for Comprehensive National Security. These two documents addressed the wealth generation and wealth protection aspects in a very comprehensive manner and identified technology as the linking factor. The fusion of these two documents has resulted in the India Millennium Missions 2020 (IMM 2020), which provides an excellent framework and road-map for making a strong and developed India by the year 2020. IMM 2020 needs Integrated actions.

## Integrated Action for Developed India

We have identified five areas where India has a core competence for an integrated action: (1) Agriculture and food processing – we have to put a target of 360 million tons of food and agricultural production. Other areas of agriculture and agrofood processing would bring prosperity to rural people and speed up the economic growth. (2) Reliable and quality electric power for all parts of the country. (3) Education and Healthcare – we have seen, based on the experience, education and healthcare are interrelated and assist population control leads to social security and also national security. (4) Information Technology – This is one of our core competence. We believe, this area can be used to promote education in remote areas and also to create national wealth. (5) Strategic sectors – This area, fortunately, witnessed the growth in nuclear technology, space technology and defence technology. These five areas are closely interrelated and lead to national, food, economic and security. A strong partnership among the R&D, academy, industry, business and the community as a whole with the Government departments and agencies will be essential to accomplish the vision.

## Empowerment

When the child is empowered by the parents, at various phases of growth, the child gets transformed into a responsible citizen. When the teacher is empowered with knowledge and experience, good young human beings with value systems take shape. When individual or a team is empowered with technology, transformation to higher potential for achievement is assured. When the leader of any institution empowers his or her people, leaders are born who can change the nation in multiple areas. When women are empowered, society with stability gets assured. When the political leaders of the nation empower the people through visionary policies, the prosperity of the nation is certain. When religion transforms into a spiritual force the people become enlightened citizens with value system.

## Concluding Remarks

While quoting Sir C.V. Raman, he said. Success can only come to you by courageous devotion to the task lying in front of you. I can assert without fear of contradiction that the quality of the Indian mind is equal to the quality of any Teutonic, Nordic or Anglo-Saxon mind. What we lack is perhaps courage, what we lack is perhaps driving force which takes one anywhere. We have, I think, developed an inferiority complex. I think what is needed in India today is the destruction of that defeatist spirit. We need a spirit of victory, a spirit that will carry us to our rightful place under the sun, a spirit which will recognise that we, as inheritors of a proud civilization, are entitled to a rightful place on this planet. If that indomitable spirit were to arise, nothing can hold us from achieving our rightful destiny."

□

*Address at the Shanmugananda Fine Arts & Sangeetha Sabha, Mumbai on 15-02-2003.*

# 14
# Three Best Teachers in My Life

## First Teacher – My Father

My father Janab Avul Pakir Jainulabdeen, as a first teacher or Guru. My father taught me a great lesson when I was a young boy. What was that lesson? It was just after India got independence. At that time panchayat board elections took place at Rameswaram. My father was elected Panchayat Board member and on the same day he was also elected the President of Rameswaram Panchayat Board. Rameswaram Island was a beautiful place with 30,000 populations. At that time they elected my father as Panchayat Board President not because he belonged to a particular religion or a particular caste or spoke a particular language or for his economic status. He was elected only on the basis of his nobility of mind and for being a good human being. I would like to narrate one incident that took place on the day he was elected President of Panchayat Board.

I was at that time studying in School. Those days we did not have electricity and we used to study under ration kerosene lamps. I was reading the lessons loudly and I heard a knock at the door. We never used to lock the door in Rameswaram in those days. Somebody opened the door, came in and asked me where my father was? I told him that father had gone for evening Namaz. Then he said, I have brought something for him, can I keep it here? Since my father had gone for Namaz, I shouted for my mother to get her permission to receive the gift. Since she was also on the Namaz there was no response. I asked the person to leave the gift on the cot. After that I continued my studies.

When my father came in and saw a *tambalum* kept in the cot. He asked me "What is this? Who has given that?" I told him, "Somebody came and has kept this for you." He opened the cover of the *tambalum* and found there was a costly *dhoti, angawastram*, some fruits and some sweets and he could see the slip that the person had left behind. I was the youngest child of my father, he really loved me and I also loved him a lot. He was upset at the sight of the *Tambalum* and gifts left some one. That was the first time I saw him very angry and also that was the first time I had got a severe beating from him. I got frightened and started weeping. My mother embraced and consoled me. "Then my father came and touched my shoulder lovingly with affection and advised me not to receive any gift in future, without his permission. He quoted an Islamic Hadith, which states that, "When the almighty appoints a person to a position, He takes care of his provision. If a person takes anything beyond that, it is an illegal gain." Then he told me that it is not a good habit. Gift is always accompanied by some purpose and a gift is a dangerous thing. It is like touching a snake and getting the poison in turn. This lesson stands out always in my mind even when I am in my seventies. This incident, taught me a very valuable lesson for my life. It is deeply embedded in my mind.

According to Manu Smriti, "By Accepting gifts the divine light in the person gets extinguished." Manu warns every individual against accepting gifts for the reason that it places the acceptor under an obligation in favour of the person who gave the gift and ultimately it results in making a person to do things which are not permitted according to law.

## My Second Teacher – Primary School Teacher Shri Siva Subramania Iyer

At the age of 13 in 8th class. I had a teacher, Shri Siva Subramania Iyer. He was one of the very good teachers in our school. All of us loved to attend his class and hear him. One day he was teaching about bird's flight. He drew a diagram of a bird on the blackboard depicting the wings, tail and the body structure with the head. He explained how the birds create the lift and fly. He also explained to us how they change direction while flying. Nearly for 25 minutes he gave the lecture with various information such as lift, drag, how the birds fly in a formation of 10, 20 or 30. At the end of the class, he wanted to know whether we understood how the birds fly. I said, I did not understand how the birds fly. When I said this, the teacher asked the other students whether they understood or not. Many students said that they also did not understand. He did not get upset by our response since he was a committed teacher.

He took all of us to the seashore. That evening the whole class was at the seashore of Rameswaram. We enjoyed the roaring sea waves knocking at the sandy hills in the pleasant evening. Birds were flying with sweet chirping voice. He showed the sea birds in formations of 10 to 20 numbers. We saw the marvellous formations of birds with a purpose and we were all amazed. He showed us the birds and asked us to see that when the birds fly, what they looked like. We saw the wings flapping. He asked us to look at the tail portion with the combination of flapping wings and twisting tail. We noticed closely and found that the birds in that condition flew in the direction they desired. Then he asked us a question, where the engine is and how it is powered. Bird is powered by its own life and the motivation of what it wants. All these things were explained to us within 15 minutes. This is real teaching. I am sure many of the teachers in schools and colleges will follow this example.

For me, it was not merely an understanding of how a bird flies. The bird's flight entered into me and created a special feeling. From that evening, I thought that my future study has to be with reference to flight and flight systems. I am saying this because my teacher's teaching and the event that I witnessed decided my future career. Then one evening after the classes, I asked the teacher, "Sir, please tell me, how to progress further in learning all about flight." He patiently explained to me that I should complete 8th class, and then go to high school, and then I should go to engineering college that may lead to education on flight. If I complete all my education with excellence, I might do something connected with flight sciences. This advice and the bird flying exercise given by my teacher, really gave me a goal and a mission for my life. When I went to college, I took Physics. When I went to engineering in Madras Institute of Technology (MIT), I took Aeronautical Engineering.

Thus my life was transformed as a rocket engineer, aerospace engineer and technologist. That one incident of my teacher teaching the lesson, showing the visual live example proved to be a turning point in my life which eventually shaped my profession.

A student during his school life upto 10+2 spends 25,000 hours in the school campus. His life is, more influenced by the teachers and the school environment. Therefore, the school must have the best of teachers with ability to, teach and love teaching and build moral qualities. Teachers should become role models. Similarly, the student must be alert to build himself with best of qualities and to get ignited with a vision for his or her future life.

## My Third Teacher – The Design Teacher Prof. Satish Dhawan

Experience with my mentor Prof. Satish Dhawan. First, I worked in Delhi with the Ministry of Defence. Later I joined Defence Research and Development Organisation (DRDO) in 1958 at Aeronautical Development Establishment at Bangalore. There with the advice of the Director, I took up the development of Hovercraft. Hovercraft design needed the development of a ducted contra-rotating propeller for creating a smooth flow balancing the torques. I did not know how to design a contra-rotating propeller though I knew how to design a conventional propeller. Some of my friends told me that I can approach Prof. Satish Dhawan of Indian Institute of Science, who was well-known for his aeronautical research, for help in designing the ducted contra-rotating propeller.

I took permission from my Director Dr. Mediratta and went to Prof. Satish Dhawan at IISc. Prof. Satish Dhawan asked me what the problem was that I would like to discuss? I explained the problem to Prof. Dhawan about my project work. He told me that it is really a challenging task and he would teach me the design if I attend his classes in IISc between 2.00 p.m. to 3.00 p.m. on all Saturdays for the next 6 weeks. He was a visionary teacher. He prepared the schedule for the entire course and wrote it on the black board. He also gave me the reference material and books I should read before I start attending the course. I considered, this as a great opportunity and I started attending the discussion and started meeting him regularly. Before commencing each meeting, he would ask critical questions and assess my understanding of the subject. That was for the first time that I realised how a good teacher prepares himself for teaching with meticulous planning and prepares the student for acquisition of knowledge. This process continued for the next six weeks. I got the capability for designing the contra-rotating propeller. Prof. Dhawan told me that I am ready for developing the contra-rotating propeller for a given hovercraft configuration. That was the time I realised that Prof. Satish Dhawan was not only a teacher but also a fantastic development engineer of aeronautical systems.

Later during the critical phases of testing Professor Dhawan was with me to witness the test and find solutions to the problems. After reaching the smooth test phase, contra-rotating propeller went through 50 hours of continuous testing. Prof. Satish Dhawan witnessed the test himself and congratulated me. That was a great day for me when I saw the contra-rotating propeller designed by my team performing to the mission requirement in the hovercraft. However, at that time, I did not realize that Prof. Satish Dhawan would become Chairman, ISRO and that I would get the opportunity to work with him as a Project Director in the development of satellite launch vehicle SLV-3 for injecting the Rohini Satellite into the orbit. Nature has its own way to link the student's dream and the real life later.

## Conclusion

The three teachers in my life what did they give me? In an integrated way it can be said, that any enlightened human being can be created by three unique characteristics. One is moral value system. That I got from my father the hard way. Secondly, the teacher becoming a role model. Not only does the student learn, but the teacher shapes his life with great dreams and aims. Finally, the education and learning process have to culminate in the creation of professional capability leading to confidence and will power to make a design, to make a product, to make a system, bravely combating many problems. What a fortune and blessing I had from my three best teachers?

□

*Address on the Eve of Teachers' Day – 2003 Broadcast on All India Radio, New Delhi on 04-09-2003.*

# 15

# Teachers' Role in Nation Building

## Put the Students, Decades Ahead

As young students, we had the opportunity at St. Joseph's College witnessing a scene, a unique, divine looking personality walking through the college campus every morning teaching Mathematics BSc (Honours) and MA (Mathematics) students. Young students looked at him with awe and respect, a personality symbolizing our own culture. When he walked, knowledge radiated all around. The great personality was, Prof.T.Totadri Iyengar, the great teacher. At that time, 'Calculus Srinivasan', was my mathematics teacher. Calculus Srinivasan used to talk about Prof. Totadri Iyengar with deep respect. During those days, he and Prof. Totadri Iyengar had an understanding to have an integrated class by Prof. Totadri Iyengar for first year B.Sc. (Hons) and first year B.Sc. (Physics). I had the opportunity to attend his classes, particularly on the subjects of modern algebra, statistics and also once I heard him teaching complex variables. When we were in the BSc first year, Calculus Srinivasan used to select top ten students to the Mathematics Club of St. Joseph's to where Prof. Totadri Iyengar used to give lecture series. One day, in 1952, I still remember, he gave a one hour lecture on ancient mathematicians and astronomers of India and introduced three great mathematician and astronomers. For nearly one hour he spoke. The lecture is still ringing in my ears. I was introduced to the pride of the nation: pioneers in astronomy and mathematics (4th to 20th century) Aryabhata, Bhaskara and Ramanujam who gave to the world, the zero, computed the orbit period of the earth around the sun and discovered many stunning concepts in number theory. These incidents and knowledge became the foundation for my education, learning with hope and value system. My teachers of primary, secondary and college education had put me a few decades ahead. This was indeed the vision. I am confident there may be many parallels in this gathering, let us emulate them. How can the students be shaped as nation builders and schools become laboratories for such type of mission?

I had an interesting experience of meeting Vice Chancellors at Hyderabad and suggesting certain questions for discussion. A professor of Texas A&M University Dr. Robert Slater, an expert in Education and Human Resource Development, further took up the question from the media, analysed and sent me an email. Later we met, discussed and evolved the capacities for nation building. This trait of analysis is noteworthy. Let it spread among the teaching community.

## Conclusion

Good teachers can generate enlightened human beings with unique characteristics of moral value and professional capabilities. Teachers can induce the confidence and will power among the students for realizing their dreams. Every one of us in this planet creates the page in human history irrespective of who he/she is. Your experiences highlighted today are the dots in human history with life and light. This light, let it light many lamps.

□

*National Awards for Teachers, New Delhi on 05-09-2003.*

# 16

# Sports: A Unifying Spirit

While participating in the closing ceremony of the first Afro-Asian Games which commenced on 24th October 2003 at Balayogi Stadium. When I see thousands of sportspersons assembled there, I realize they have come from large number of countries and represent more than half of the population of this planet. When youth and dynamic action are combined through sports, I am sure these sportspersons will electrify the continents by their creativity and innovation and above all by their sweat and excellent performance. The combined power of the youth ignited by the spirit of sportsmanship will be the most powerful resource of all resources on the earth, above the earth and under the earth.

I appreciate the excellent spirit of the Government and people of Andhra Pradesh who have been the gracious hosts for this great event and made all the participants feel at home at Hyderabad. I would like to congratulate all the organizers for providing a platform and making excellent arrangements to conduct this mega event with clockwork precision. I also commend the efforts and contribution of the parents, teachers, coaches and various agencies in motivating the sportspersons to reach the heights of their performance and for providing an environment of encouragement and adequate challenge.

Different ideas, value systems and ways of living are amalgamating to create a new world. In this new global community, the human spirit will rule over the management of the mind. Amidst sportspersons from Africa and Asia, a gathering that has happened for the first time in the history, I can feel the arrival of a new emerging world order.

The sportspersons who participated in Afro-Asian Games gave spectacular performance in their events, created happiness for themselves, to the fellow sportspersons, to the country, to the continent and to the entire world. All of you collectively have enriched our life. When you were toiling hard to bring laurels to your countries, the whole world was watching with interest to see how the sportspersons are putting their best to excel in their fields and create new records. While I congratulate all the medal winners, I also appreciate the performance of all the participants who have put their best to improve their performance and generated a spirit of healthy competition.

With the experience of national games and followed by First Afro-Asian Games we are graduating to meet the bigger sports challenges for conducting Commonwealth and Olympic Games in India. The experience of Afro-Asian games what we have witnessed definitely will provide the capability for all of you to compete with confidence and win medals at the Olympics. I wish that every Afro-Asian must make an entry in the medals tally in the Olympics.

If at all in human life there is any aspect that can enrich the mind, body and spirit in an integrated way, it is sports and games? I am sure all the participants will return with sweet memories of this event and will propagate the unifying spirit of universal harmony and brotherhood.

□

---

*Address at the Closing Ceremony of the First Afro-Asian Games, Hyderabad on 01-11-2003.*

# 17
# Dimensions of Creativity

## Creativity Changes Life Pattern

What we have seen in science and technology in the last 60 years, the predictions and happenings are going at different rates and phases. What was impossible has happened and what is thought possible has not yet happened and it will happen. Particularly in the field of aeronautics, space technology, electronics, materials, computer science and software products, the world has progressed to new dimensions and India itself is a part of these challenges. Indian biotechnologists with business houses will have opportunity of analyzing the available genomic data and lead to production of drugs for healthcare and early treatment. The bioresearch transforming into technology will lead to higher production of agricultural products. In the coming decades, we may see the birth of unified field theory integrating gravitational forces, electromagnetic forces and general relativity theory, space and time as functions.

On the successful completion of Moon Mission in 1961, Farnbraun, a very famous rocket designer, who built Saturn-V, to launch the capsule with astronauts and made moon walk a reality, in 1975 said? If I am authorised, I will remove the word impossible?

## Impossibility to Possibility

Human flight is nothing but creativity of human mind

and it undergoes several struggles to achieve excellence. In 1890, a great well-known scientist Lord Kelvin, who was the President of Royal Socicty of London said, anything heavier than air cannot fly, and cannot be flown? With in two decades Wright Brothers proved man could fly of course at heavy risk and cost.

## Creative Indians

In India many innovation and creative thinking took place at various phases of our development. Dr. Vikram Sarabhai in 1960s said that India should design and develop large satellite launch vehicle and put communication satellite and remote sensing satellite in geosynchronous orbit and polar orbit respectively. In India this was thought impossible. But this vision statement ignited hundreds of scientist, technologists and thousands of technicians. Today India is capable of building any type of satellite launch vehicles and satellites.

Similarly during 1960s, I remember that India was in a ship to mouth existence for foodgrains. If the American ships do not bring wheat, there will be a famine in India. But there were two visionaries who worked together with the farming community and brought the first green revolution. They are the political thinker Shri. C. Subramaniam and the agriculture scientist Dr. M.S. Swaminathan. Today we produce two hundred million tonnes of foodgrains, which is not only sufficient for us but we can also export some quantity.

Till 1953, it was thought that it was impossible to reach the Mount Everest. Hillary and Tenzing disproved this impossibility. Let us take Raman Effect; till Sir C.V. Raman found the molecular scattering, the people did not know why the sea appears to be blue. Similarly, Chandrasekhar Subramaniam, discovered that many stars shine and few don't, thereby he proved the Chandrasekhar Limit, which enabled him to discover the Black Hole.

In India 1960s, none of us dreamt that the nuclear energy can lead to electric power generation or nuclear medicine will be used for the treatment of thyroid disorder and cancer cure. Indias Homi Bhabhas vision led to the electric energy generated by nuclear power flowing into grid. Within another decade, it may increase to more than 20,000 MW of power.

## Conclusion

Your creative mind is very powerful. Ignited mind is the most powerful resource on the earth, above the earth and under the earth.

□

---

*Address During the National Bal Shree Awards for 2002 and 2003, Ashok Hall, Rashtrapati Bhavan, New Delhi on 10-02-2004.*

# 18

# Nation Smiles

"When guns are silent, Flowers blossom on the earth Fragrance engulfs good souls. Who created beautiful silence?"

## Water Mission

In his address on international conference on Water Management at Vigyan Bhavan. As you all know water is the essence of life. Water brings prosperity. Internationally out of 6 billion people, today only 2 billion get adequate water. As most of the nations are busy with their national and international problems such as wars, terrorism etc., the potential threat of water shortage in the coming years is not fully realised by them. Since most of the rivers are flowing through many nations, they could generate international disputes. We discussed two solutions with the international community on India's possible plan of action: one is the interlinking of rivers which you are fully aware of, and the other, desalination of sea water using solar energy; a new thought especially since we are blessed with seas on all three sides of our country and also possess adequate relevant technologies. International community has fully acknowledged this as the right solution not only for India but also for the global community.

## Children's Dream

Also a very interesting event happened at the same

venue. Suddenly about 200 children made me to sit with them and interact for 20 minutes. During the interaction, I asked the children what they would like to do after their 10+2 study. Many said, they want to become engineers, doctors, fashion designers, lawyers etc., Then surprisingly I found, in that gathering one boy and one girl lifted their hands simultaneously to tell me that they want to become political leaders. I asked them why they want to become political leaders? You will be happy to know the type of answer I got. The boy said, as a political leader I can give a vision to go to different planets and bring wealth to the country. There is nothing wrong in dreaming. But we have to work for it. The girl student said, she wants to become a political leader, to clean up the whole political system, particularly of corruption.

## Creativity

When my mind was hovering continuously on the children's dream and the future water problem, two pleasant things happened on the same evening. One artist, Prof. S.V. Ramarao, from south who had settled down in America and is well-known particularly for modern paintings, met me. He narrated his lifetime experience. The artist went to Europe, and he studied European paintings. He made up his mind that he wanted to excel in the European modern paintings. He worked continuously for two years and generated a series of paintings. He brought Picasso and Glandstine in his paintings. He created a newer set of western paintings with the Indian touch of colour. Every one who had seen this was astonished and never failed to admire his creativity. Today he is one of the recognised artists in the world and a great painter.

## Expanding Roles of the Rajya Sabha

Over the last 50 years the Rajya Sabha had played a critical role in addressing some of the major societal issues concerning relationships between some sections of the society, especially judiciary, women welfare, healthcare, property, behaviour etc. These are very well articulated in many of the well treasured publications of the Rajya Sabha and have had salutary effects on our post independence society.

## Field of Attention

With the passage of time, the compelling needs of the nation and the geopolitical environment have also changed. The emphasis today has shifted towards solving issues in economic development, geopolitics, world trade, national security, energy and water security, growth of agriculture, manufacturing and services in the backdrop of the emerging global village and advances in science and technologies that follow the law of accelerating returns.

UN has to be transformed into a powerful international organization with the voice heard from small or big nations, rich or poor nations. These issues are intricately intertwined with the national development. There are also problems of global violence taking many forms, including terrorism and intolerance between individuals and groups.

## Freedom to Live

One of the important characteristics of democracy is tolerance for criticism. Analysis of criticism leads to understanding of truth. Normally only criticism brings reality. Based on my visits to many parts of the country and exposure to the field problems, I find that there is a need for faster economic development in certain States. If committed people have to work selflessly, we have to ensure their safety without which their families and brethren will not allow them nor want them to work in such an uncertain environment. Freedom to move, freedom to think and freedom to express are ingrained in the freedom to live; it is also enshrined in our constitution. We cannot have interstate barriers or interregional curbs that would snap the thread of unity. All of us will have to work together to create a conducive atmosphere for unhindered progress of developmental activities.

Creating a standardised quality education with value system across the population or even creating a corruption free society are the problems that are challenging enough to demand out of the box unusual solutions. A fair and equitable access to judicial systems that are sensitive to changes in technology and society, pollution free and energy efficient urban transport systems that are scalable nation-wide are also equally challenging problems that need immediate attention. Rajya Sabha can be an architect leading to providing practical solutions during the debate. Such decisions will be the typical bricks that would be necessary to build the edifice of developed nation by 2020.

## Rajya Sabha next Two Decades

The major problems and issues of the 21st Century are emerging as highly interministry, interdepartmental, interstate matters. The Ministries, Departments and States should be able to work cohesively in a borderless way for each mission. This is much the same way that today's Internet, Intranet and Extranet all work in a coalition of convenience to create Virtual Organizations depending on the problem to be solved. In addition, since private investors and entrepreneurs will participate, we need to involve them as partners. The institutions of the State should aim to become partners of entrepreneurs and friends of citizens. Coherence and congruence in national and State development policies in the 21st century can come about only by a well-debated long-term vision for the nation as a whole, implemented efficiently and effectively by multiple interinstitutional and interdisciplinary missions, programmes and projects. Most of them for e.g. the national river water mission, Providing Urban Amenities and Rural Areas (PURA) and other suggested five areas are highly complex, technically and managerially; and they involve complex relations between Centre and States, private entities, citizens and indeed with other nations as well.

## Missions for Vision 2020

Vision 2020 has been generally accepted by the nation, now the time has come to transform the vision into mission. Vision 2020 implementation needs to be viewed as set of joint centre-state-industry-academy people missions. These include Socio-economic missions such as Interlinking of Rivers, Providing Urban Amenities to Rural Areas (PURA), Healthcare, Electrical power. Techno economic missions such as large scale use of solar and other Non-conventional Energy Sources and Socio-technical missions such as Low Intensity Conflict Management and Information Security.

For these missions, the nodal agency for individual missions may have to be carefully planned without following the current methods of departmental compartmentalization. The empowered management structure, innovative systems of execution, public accountability etc. would need to be conceptualised, debated upon, designed and implemented.

Our parliamentarians and legislatures are given local area development scheme fund which in a plan period amounts to over ₹ 15,000 crores. My careful study and analysis indicate that in India we have adequate resources. We suffer from a system of implementation, which requires to be made economically efficient. Benefits will then reach the people. For example, I suggest the honourable members should become facilitators for executing the PURA projects through these funds in their regions, which will bring visible development changes in their constituencies and meet the aspirations of the people. All these will also lead to greater employment generation and more efficient and effective governance, not necessarily in the traditional sense of job but often as self-employed skilled persons.

Every Honourable members become the ambassadors for these missions and make the one billion people participate in the noble task of, 'Developed India Movement'.

## Conclusion

Ours is a vast country – a subcontinent. As it happens with any such large country, there are multiplicities of everything, the language, religion or even ethnicities. Even natural resources are strewn across the country far and wide. If one area is rich in a particular resource, another is in another and yet another is in still another. If one area is excellent for agriculture, another is excellent for information technology, another in manufacturing and so on. All these diversities not withstanding, we Indians all along have been genuinely proud of our innate unity, our heritage and our civilization. In fact that has been the singular reason for our having been able to hold ourselves together as a proud nation with the glorious past looking forward to a still more glorious future of developed India by 2020: a happy, prosperous and safe India.

## Righteousness

"Where there is righteousness in the heart,
There is beauty in the character.
Where there is beauty in the character,
There is harmony in the home.
Where there is harmony in the home,
There is an order in the nation.
Where there is an order in the nation,
There is peace in the world."

□

---

*Inaugural Address at the 200th Session of the Rajya Sabha, New Delhi on 11-12-2003.*

# 19

# Youth and Dynamic Action

"I have now a dream,
Dream for action; Dream for performance,
I will sweat for excellence, thereby I will bring glory to the nation."

I am sure this short poem will enter into your mind to ignite the large potential in you to give the best performance. If you use this short poem, if you enter this short poem in your mind I am sure your potential for the best performance will get enhanced and you perform well.

"If at all in human life there is any aspect that can enrich the mind and body in an integrated way it is sports and games."

Parents and teachers should encourage the children to actively participate in sports and games from childhood. Children spent 25,000 hours in their school from 1st Standard to 12th Standard. Therefore, this is the place where we have to reinforce sports and games facilities to mould and encourage the growth of excellent sportspersons.

India with its billion and more population, the time has come to generate and create players and sportspersons in every area. We have to select the best performers, train them physically and mentally from childhood. We should enlist 1000 persons every year in the sports stream throughout the country. We have to educate and nurture them professionally to make sports grades, so that they can compete in Asian games and Olympics and establish a record in every event when they grow.

It has been heartening to note that our sportspersons have been toiling hard to bring laurels for the country in various international events. Very recently our sportspersons did us proud in the Asian Games 2002, when they returned with a haul of 35 medals, 10 of them gold. The performance of the Indian contingent in the 17th Commonwealth games held in August this year at Manchester was quite historic. Our young sportspersons returned with 69 medals, India securing 4th position in these games. These achievements were basically due to their dedication, commitment and unflinching desire to excel in the international arena.

A sportsperson gets evolved for superior performance in an environment where there is physical, psychological and nutritional support. We have to scientifically develop athletes and sportspersons to have maximum lung volume, muscle power, endurance and metabolic profile by intensive training from childhood. I am sure the Centre and all states will evolve the development of sports and games as an integrated effort from childhood to adulthood. The parents, teachers and the society need to provide an ambience to encourage the children to achieve the high level of performance in sports and athletics.

□

---

*Address at the Inauguration of the National Games 2002, Hyderabad on 13-12-2002.*

# 20

# When can I Sing the Song of India?

The best artistes of our nation were giving their best symbiotically converging with each other. I was moved; we were moved and the whole nation moved. Can we give the best in our field, like them? If we, the billion people, give our best in each one's task, no one on this planet can stop India from achieving its developed nation status – with economic prosperity, peace and happiness – a state that will make every Indian sing the song of India.

## Dynamics of Warfare

For a decade I was studying the dynamics of warfare on the planet earth. It is evident that man lives on wars. We distinctly see that warfare has three parts: upto 1920, 1920-1990, after 1990. The first part was human warfare period. Motivation for human warfare was either territorial greediness or wealth ambitions or religious domination which in combination later led to the First World War. The second period, 1920-1990 – was a mechanical warfare period. During this period the world graduated to use of new mechanised weapons and platforms – battle tanks, fighter aircrafts and submarines. The motivation was ideological conflicts between two societies. Second World War also witnessed the disaster by the deployment of nuclear bombs on two cities of Japan. During the third period from 1990 we see market warfare and globalisation. The tool used is the supremacy of the technology which led to technology denials and control regimes separating the nations as 'Developed', 'Developing' and 'Under Developed'. In 2003, the world is facing a new kind of warfare, due to integrated situation of religious conflicts, ideological differences and market warfare. We have witnessed always that war adds to wars, of course there will be a time gap. We are witnessing today an unilateral war waged against Iraq. This situation has weakened the world body, United Nations. This situation need to be properly analysed for remedial action. How do we combat these complex integrated phenomena of conventional warfare threat, cross border terrorism, insurgency and threat of nuclear attacks? Remedies off there problems are given below:

## Our Civilisational Heritage

Nation of billion people thinking like nation of million people. Why is it so? Whereas Indians are natural born leaders in critical situations and challenging environments for the reason they live in a society of multi religious and multiethnical groups. I consider no other nation like India, has got the civilisational heritage to live near peaceful life. Indian minds were capable of absorbing the best of cultures from the successive invasions. We have also evolved the great qualities of leadership to manage the nation of billion people with various dimensions in every aspect of life. Now we should not allow any religion or any individual fanaticism to endanger our nation. Because, nation is very important compared to any individual or party or religion.

## India through Ages

India had its glory during early civilization and agricultural age. Successive invasions and foreign rules and rise in population brought down India's prosperity to a lower level. India also could not participate in the Industrial Revolution which led the western countries to take a lead, increasing the gap between the West and India. India went through famine, starvation in many parts and national calamities and looked for ships to come to our ports with wheat from western countries. After Independence, India looked forward in development through Five Year Plans. The Green Revolution and the technology growth enabled India to prosper with self-sufficiency in food and achievement in many technological frontiers particularly during the last two decades. A major transformation came during the information age where India established its position with its strong core competence in Information Technology. Today India is in the knowledge age which will provides an opportunity to become a developed nation with strong economy (IT).

## Economic Growth in Different Societies

During the last century, the world has undergone a change from agriculture society, where manual labour was the critical factor, to industrial society where the management of technology, capital and labour provided the competitive advantage. Then the information era was born in the last decade, where connectivity and software products are driving the economy of a few nations. In the 21st century, a new society is emerging where knowledge is the primary production resource instead of capital and labour. Efficient utilisation of this existing knowledge can create comprehensive wealth of the nation and also improve the quality of life – in the form of better health, education, infrastructure and other social indicators. Ability to create and maintain the knowledge infrastructure, develop knowledge workers and enhance their productivity through creation, growth and exploitation of new knowledge will be the key factors in deciding the prosperity of this Knowledge Society. Whether a nation has arrived at a stage of knowledge society is judged by the way the country effectively deals with knowledge creation and knowledge deployment in all sectors like IT, Industries, Agriculture, Health Care etc.

## Changes in Employment, Agriculture, Industry and Service – Knowledge Industries

In 1980, agriculture areas employed in parts or in full 76% of people of the country and it reduced to 65% in 1994 and expected to further fall to 60% of people in agriculture by 2012. Whereas, the demand of agricultural products will be double in quantity, productivity using technology and post harvest management will have to compensate the manpower reduction in farming and agricultural products sector. In the case of industry, in 1980, 13% of the population was employed in small-scale and large-scale industries. The trend continued during 1994. However, it has to increase in 2010, as the GDP growth with high technology in the situation of opening up of the economy under WTO regime. The pattern of employment will take a new shape. Service with knowledge industry component from 11% employability in 1980 has increased to 20% in 1994. And further it will increase to 54% in 2012 in view of infrastructure, maintenance areas, financial sector, IT sector and entertainment demands. This big change will demand in all areas more trained skilled human power and technology personnel. Our industrialists, commercial chiefs and technologists may have to get ready for such transformation in agriculture, industries and service – knowledge industries for which human manpower with knowledge and skills has to be evolved in a mission mode. And also evolution of knowledge management has been presented linking vision for the nation.

Providing Urban Amenities in Rural Areas (PURA) is another example for creating rural wealth and prosperity. The model envisages a habitat designed to improve the quality of life in rural places and makes special suggestions to remove urban congestion also. Naturally our most demanding urban problem is that of congestion removal and efficient supply of water and effective waste disposal in every locality are thc paramount civic needs. There is a minimum size below which a habitat is not viable and not competitive with the existing congested city. At the same time, the existing congested city is not economical compared to a new town once a minimum size of expansion is crossed. As against a conventional city say, rectangular in shape and measuring approximately 10 km by 6 km, the model considers an annular ring-shaped town integrating minimum 8 to 10 villages of the same 60 $km^2$ area. This model provides easy access to villages, saves transportation time and cuts costs substantially and is more convenient for general public. Knowledge powered rural development is an essential need for transforming India into a knowledge power and high bandwidth rural connectivity is the minimum requirement to take education, health care and economic activities to the rural areas. Knowledge society leading to knowledge superpower can prosper and survive only in the environment of economic security and internal security. Physical connectivity by providing roads, electronic connectivity by providing reliable communication network and knowledge connectivity by establishing professional institutions and vocational training centers will have to be done in an integrated way so that economic connectivity will emanate. Such model of establishing a circular connectivity among the rural village complexes will accelerate rural development process by empowerment.

## Prosperous, Happy and Peaceful India

The nation's strengths predominantly reside in its natural and human resources. In natural resources, India is endowed with a vast coastline with marine resources and also oil wealth. In minerals, apart from conventional material resources, it is well-known that India has the largest deposits of titanium, beryllium and tungsten. India ranks among the top few nations having a rich biodiversity. Knowledge-based value addition for these natural resources would mean exporting value-added products rather than merely the raw materials. Use of IT for commercialisation and marketing can increase our outreach and speed enormously. Ancient knowledge is a unique resource of India for it has the treasure of a minimum of 5000 years of civilisation. It is essential to leverage this wealth for national well-being as well as to seek global presence for the nation. Civilisation that does not have the knowledge of technology or the technological nations without experience of civilisation, cannot innovate newer economy. Human resources, particularly with large young population, are unique core strength of the nation. This resource can be transformed through various educational and training programmes. Skilled, unskilled and creative manpower can be transformed into wealth generators particularly in the service sectors, agro industries etc. Knowledge-intensive industries can be generated out of our existing industries by injecting demand for high-level software/ hardware, which would bring tremendous value addition. It is said, "The precious asset for a company or a country is the skill, ingenuity and imagination of its people. With globalisation, this will become more important because everybody will have access to world class technology and the key distinguishing feature will be the ability of people in different countries to use their imagination to make the best use of the technology." Indeed development and innovative use of multiple technologies with mission projects and transparent management structure will catapult India into a, 'developed nation'.

## Creative Leadership

For building the developed India, what are needed? We have natural resources and we have human power. There are 700 million people below 35 years in the population of a billion people. The nation needs young leaders who can command the change for transformation of India into a developed nation embedded with knowledge society from now to twenty years. The leaders are the creators of new organizations of excellence. Quality leaders are like magnets that will attract the best of persons to build the team for the organization and give inspiring leadership even during failures of missions as they are not afraid of risks.

One of the very important ingredients for success of the vision of transforming India into a developed nation by 2020 is the evolution of creative leaders. I am giving a connectivity between developed India, economic prosperity, technology, production, productivity, employee role and management quality, all of which linked to the creative leader. Who is that creative leader? What are the qualities of a creative leader? The creative leadership is exercising the task to change the traditional role from commander to coach, manager to mentor, from director to delegator and from one who demands respect to one who facilitate self-respect. The higher the proportion of creative leaders in a nation, the higher the potential of success of visions like 'Developed India'.

## Conclusion

India has demonstrated its immense capabilities and core-competence to the world with large talented manpower. It is a nuclear weapon state, self-sufficient in space efforts and defense research, could able to combat technology denial regimes, largest producer of milk, self-sufficient in food, leading in pharmaceuticals, competent in Information Technology and has large natural resources. What else we need?

□

---

*38th Convocation Address at Indian Institute of Management, Ahmedabad on 29-03-2003.*

# 21
# Universal Unity and Understanding

## Four Noble Truths

University of Universal Unity and Understanding should experience four noble truths. What are the four noble truths, you are all philosophers, theologists, thinkers, and may be tourism marketers also, you know what are those truths. However, I felt that I should narrate these noble truths, which are ringing in my mind in divine form, where Buddha got enlightenment.

The first truth is Dukkha, which states that the world is transient and it is in Dukkha. The second truth is the root cause of Dukkha, desire (Samudaya). If we eliminate desire dukkha will cease, is the third truth (Nirodha). Fourth is to follow the Eight-Fold Path (Magga).

## Nalanda the University of Enlightenment

I would like to narrate the incident which took place in Nalanda, when I was there in May 2003. I have spent hours and hours in Nalanda. I saw the place, where the hundreds of scholars assembled and discoursed. I saw, how a university was vibrant in the Nalanda area in 7th and 8th century with theology-teaching classrooms, discourse rooms and monks hostels. What attracted the scholars from 90 countries to Nalanda long ago? This is the place where the thoughts were transmitted, discussed and integrated towards a good way of life, which people were looking for from many countries. Friends, at this critical juncture of universal turbulence and instability, arising out of mutual distrust and hatred leading to violence, world needs a university of peace, enlightenment and great thoughts.

After enlightenment Buddha walked and walked in 45 different places in and around Nalanda, Bihar and Uttar Pradesh. Every place is very important for Spiritual enlightenment. To commemorate this great event, it is essential to re-establish a university in Nalanda, dedicated to the philosophy of Buddha to cherish and find new meaning – A University of Universal Unity and Understanding. I would suggest this conclave can give a recommendation and the Ministry of HRD, Ministry of Tourism and Culture can spearhead the establishment of this University of Universal Unity and Understanding. Now I would like to share with you some of my personal experiences in search of unity of minds.

## Experience at Bodh Gaya

What a great experience? When I visited Bodh Gaya and sat under the great Bodhi Tree with monks assembled all around. I said, *Buddham Saranam Gachami*? It was echoing every where, this I did after visiting the great Buddhist temple where Buddha was radiating peace and enlightenment. Under the holy tree a discussion started. One young monk asked me? Mr. President, President of India you are sitting in the place of great enlightenment. How do you feel? I told them, that I felt, as though I am a student, looking for a message for the troubled world – the message of peace. Another young monk asked me, Do you think Mr. President, Is Buddhism a religion or spiritual force or a code of conduct? I said, let me share with you my experiences after my extensive travel in our country and abroad.

## Religion Transforming into Spirituality

A message, I have received is that most Indians experienced and old, energetic and middle-aged, young and innocent, they all look to religion for solace and safety. I have also visited great many religious places and houses of worship throughout the length and breadth of this great country and I have met many of our religious leaders. The religions are like exquisite gardens, places full of surpassing beauty and tranquillity, like sacred groves filled with beautiful birds and their melodious songs. I truly think that religions are beautiful gardens. They are enchanting islands, veritable oasis for the soul and the spirit. But they are islands nevertheless. How can we connect them so that the fragrance engulfs the whole universe? If we can connect all the islands with love and compassion, in a 'garland', we will have a prosperous India and prosperous world. With this background, I have come to Bodh Gaya. I realize in Buddhism spiritual content is very high.

## Strength and Peace

The third question – a very important question was asked by the youngest monk. Mr. President you have made a weapon, which can carry a nuclear warhead and you are in search for peace now? How they are compatible? I was taken aback. I went back to 2500 years in history. I saw in front of me the Emperor Asoka conquering all parts of India and walking with great pride. When he came to Kalinga region, the great Kalinga war took place, which is now in the present state of Orissa. With the mighty army of Emperor Asoka fought and fought and the Kalinga kings were defeated. Emperor Asoka happily proclaimed and annexed the Kalinga country. In that great full moon night, with the success behind him, Emperor Asoka walked in the war ravaged battlefield. He stopped suddenly and saw the blood flowing over hundred thousand people who were killed, and many souls crying and moaning. That crying was engulfed with gloom. Suddenly Emperor Asoka stopped and asked himself, O! Almighty, what have I done? This spark of thought entered into the mind and soul of Emperor Asoka and the great principle of *Ahimsa, Dharma* was born.

He has preached *ahimsa,* since then. This has been firmly engraved in the mountains. In the last century Mahatma Gandhi further gave a new dimension to *ahimsa, dharma* in the freedom movement of India. I have given this answer to that young monk. In our case, it was self-defence for which nuclear weapons were developed and nation had to become a nuclear weapon country. At no time, we will use them, unless someone uses against us. If every nation possessing nuclear weapons decides to dismantle completely, India will be the first to do so. India has always been advocating a total disarmament in the world.

The fourth question was asked by another monk, Mr. President, what made you to come to Bodh Gaya? I said, I am like Anand in a small way I am in the mission of search, where is the universal peace and unity of minds?

## Experience at RILA Monastery

During my recent visit abroad, I visited a Christian Monastery in RILA located in the hills of Bulgaria. It is the biggest Bulgarian revival, spiritual and cultural centre with a 16,000 volume library including 134 manuscripts from 15th to 19th century. This holy site played an important role in the spiritual and social life of medieval Bulgaria. Destroyed by fire due to invasion at the beginning of the 19th century, the complex was rebuilt later and is now surrounded by a big fort. While being in that divine environment amidst the Reverent Fathers aged between 80 and 90, I felt like praying. I went to the altar and asked permission of the Reverent Bishop John to recite the part of the prayer of St. Francis of Assisi. All the people present in the Monastery repeated the prayer.

## The Prayer of St. Francis of Assisi

"Lord, make me an instrument of Your peace;
Where there is hatred let me sow love;
And where there is injury, pardon;
And where there is doubt, faith;
And where there is despair, hope;
And where there is darkness, light;
and where there is sadness, joy."

The silent message in this prayer was felt by the Reverent Bishop, who blessed me by saying You work for world peace.

## Celebrating the beauty of other religion

On one occasion, as I was leaving for Bangalore, I spoke to a friend of mine and told him that I would be talking to young people and whether he had any suggestions. He did not offer any suggestions as such but offered me these nuggets of wisdom.

When you speak, speak the truth; perform when you promise; discharge your trust withhold your hands from striking and from taking that which is unlawful and bad.

What actions are most excellent? To gladden the heart of a human being, to feed the hungry to help the affected, to lighten the sorrow of the sorrowful and to remove the wrongs of the injured.

All Gods creatures are his family; and he is the most beloved of God who tries to do most good to Gods creatures.

These are the sayings of Prophet Mohammad. My friend who told me this is a great grandson of a Deekshidar of Tamil Nadu and grandson of a Ganapadigal (Vedic Scholar). He is none other than Shri Y.S. Rajan.

## My Search

We had witnessed the First World War, the Second World War; the UN was created to prevent war and bring peace. But what is happening now? We all very well know that ignoring United Nations many wars are being launched on this planet. Take our case, in our nation nearly 50 years we have been experiencing cross-border terrorism. It has been causing death and suffering more than a war. This pain is in my mind. Hu Shih, (1891-1962), Chinese philosopher in Republican China has said, "India conquered and dominated China culturally for two thousand years without ever having to send a single soldier across her border." This is what Buddhist culture can do bring people together, bring nations together, and bring peace at no cost. This is religion that had grown in stature to be the Messiah of God and the advocate of the spiritual role of the religion. When the spiritual role of the religion is compromised, the religion becomes a weapon of destruction and a divider of people.

I am completely convinced that the religions can come out of dogmas. There is a possibility of religions graduating into a spiritual force with the use of compassion and love as a bridge. For sustainable societal peace and happiness, two more things are essential, one is Education with value system and the other is bringing economic prosperity. Education with value system definitely a big mission, it needs a world body, all the youth in the world, up to the age of 20, has to be taught the education with value system.

## Education with Value System

The best part of a young person is his or her childhood in school and the best time spent is 0800 Hrs to 1600 Hrs in the school. The prime learning environment is 5th to 16th years of age. The student spends approximately 25,000 hours in the school campus. Of course, at home, love and affection are imparted but again most of the time of the day is spent in preparing schools home work and study, eat, play and sleep. Hence the school hours for children are the best time for learning and need best of environment, mission-oriented learning with value system. I still hear the echo from Bestolozzy, a great teachers saying, give me a child for seven years. Afterwards, let the God or devil take the child. They cannot change the child. That is the great confidence of the teacher. What a golden mission a school can have. All the more, the teachers are in the center of the mission. We need hundreds and thousands and lakhs of committed teachers, who can shape the minds of our youth. Technology can also play a vital role to propagate good teaching through teleeducation. The best of dynamic triangle is child, teacher and parents. For parents and teachers, school campus and home have to have an integrated mission: education with value system. If the child misses the value-based education in the school, no government or society can establish a transparent society or a society with integrity.

The Nations will target development milestones in a spirited environment instead of spending tremendous energy and time in problems initiated by small aims. This is the essential environment need for transforming India into a developed nation.

**Developed India: 2020**

The most vital component for peace is the poverty eradication by attaining economic prosperity resulting in high employment potential. This model will vary from nation-to-nation depending on the core competence of the particular nation. This will be through the second vision for the nation. How we can prepare ourselves to this challenge?

To become a developed India, the essential needs are (a) India has to be economically and commercially powerful, at least to be one of the four top nations in terms of size of the economy. Our target should be a sustained GDP growth of 10% annually for a decade and that the people below poverty line to be reduced to near zero from 260 millions. Technology Vision 2020 is the roadmap to realize this cherished mission.

The vision identifies five core areas for an integrated action. They are (1) Agriculture and food processing – The target of 360 million tons of food from the present 200 million tons and creation of food processing industries with enhanced productivity. Other areas of agriculture and agro-food processing would bring prosperity to rural people and speed up the economic growth. (2) Reliable and quality electric power for all parts of the country. (3) Education and Healthcare – we have seen, based on one experience, education and healthcare are interrelated. (4) Information Communication Technology – This is one of our core competencies. We believe, this area can be used to promote education in remote areas and also to create national wealth. (5) Strategic sectors – This area, fortunately, witnessed the growth in nuclear technology, space technology and defence technology and we have further programmes in critical technologies.

The integrated action on these five mission areas will lead to economic prosperity for the nation. For ensuring peace in the world every nation has to have economic prosperity. The value based education and religion transforming into spirituality are the other vital ingredients for generating enlightened citizen in a nation.

## Conclusion

The message to the world is create enlightened citizens through the University of Universal Unity and Understanding. In short the mission of an university based on the Nalanda experience is to attract many scholars, religious leaders and scientists from various parts of the world to discourse, discuss and spread the message of love and compassion through the three principles of Education with value-system, religion transforming into spiritual force and economic development for freedom from hunger through a three-dimensional approach. India with one billion people representing one sixth of the world population has the responsibility to initiate this movement of creating enlightened citizens of the world for ensuring world peace.

□

*Address at the Inauguration of the International Conclave on Buddhism and Spiritual Tourism Vigyan Bhavan, New Delhi on 17-02-2004.*

# 22

# Evolution of a Beautiful India

## Indian Economic Scenario

Indian economy shows a very robust and consistent growth. Our foreign exchange reserves have crossed the $100 billion mark and are continuously rising. The rupee is steady and the middle class resurgence and the domestic buying power are on the rise. This has made our economy one of the fastest growing in the world. The time has come for these economic benefits to reach speedily the rural population through development programmes such as PURA. Providing Urban Amenities in Rural Areas and Interlinking of Rivers. Economists all around the world predict that by the year 2020, the world economic scenario will be completely different from what it is today, and that India will occupy the pride of position.

Indian industries in certain sectors have matured to be very responsive to the national and international needs and have shown steady growth in spite of earlier adverse predictions. Interest rates from the banks need to be more proactive to stimulate the growth of the right type of small, medium scale industry and agrofood processing industries. The combination of entrepreneurship education in the schools and colleges, the hassle free flow of venture capital and evolution of good market will give additional momentum for national growth.

## Transforming India into a Competitive Beautiful Nation

In the next five years, with certain progress behind us, the challenge we have, is to launch a major thrust for attaining national prosperity. We should convert the present opportunity and work towards giving our future generations, a competitive nation which has the following characteristics.

## Profile of Competitive India

(a) A Nation that is prosperous, healthy, secure, peaceful and happy.

(b) A Nation where the rural and urban divide has reduced to a thin line.

(c) A Nation where there is an equitable distribution of energy and quality water.

(d) A Nation where agriculture, industry and service sector work together in symphony, absorbing technology thereby resulting in sustained wealth generation leading to higher employment potential.

(e) A Nation where education is not denied to any meritorious candidates because of societal or economic discrimination.

(f) A Nation which is the best destination for the most talented scholars and scientists all over the world.

(g) A Nation where the best of health care is available to all the billion population and the diseases like AIDS/TB, water borne diseases, cardiac diseases and cancer are extinct.

(h) A Nation where the governance uses the best of the technologies to be responsive, transparent, easily accessible and simple in rules, thereby corruption-free.

(i) A Nation where poverty has been totally alleviated, illiteracy and crime against women are eradicated and the society is unalienated.

(j) A Nation that is one of the best places to live in, on the earth and brings smiles on a billion faces.

These are the ten dimensional transformations needed for a competitive India and we have to work for.

## Peace in the Offing

For continuing our mission of national development and economic growth in our subcontinent, peace is a paramount ingredient. Most nations have realised that low intensity proxy wars, deterrence-based build-ups and real wars are too expensive detractors from the perceived visions of development. The development of the society also weans away its people from destructive activities of alienation, leading to celebration of peace-makers.

"When guns are silent,
Flowers blossom on the earth;
Fragrance engulfs good souls,
Who created beautiful silence."

India will always be grateful to the successful peace-makers.

## Towards Unity of Minds

When I assumed office on 25th July 2002, I addressed the need for unity of minds becoming one of the focused missions for our nation. Recently fifteen Gurus, Acharyas, Swamijis, Maulavis, Reverent Fathers, Spiritual leaders, devotees and the representatives of many religions met at Surat in the presence of His Holiness Acharya Mahaprajna and deliberated for two days and took vital decisions leading to the religions graduating as spiritual force. Also, they have declared that the nation is bigger than any leader or individual or an organization. They had collectively evolved five inter-religious projects for implementation. Nations best wishes to our spiritual leaders and their mission of transforming religions into a spiritual force.

## Challenges Before Us

Also certain challenges before the nation are to be addressed collectively in the immediate future to facilitate faster pace of national development.

**Service to Society:** Our scientists should become civic scientists and contribute towards societal transformation. Civic means concerning or affecting the community or the people. In the new capacity, scientists step beyond their campuses, laboratories, ministries and institutes and move into the center of their communities to engage in active dialogue and action with their fellow citizens. They should ask themselves a question, how their knowledge can make an impact on the common mans life? Our civil servants and others in the service sector should become fearlessly people-friendly, have a positive attitude, and provide responsive, proactive, transparent and unbiased administration and service to the billion people.

**Primary Education:** Assent has been accorded for the 86th Constitution Amendment Act? Right to Education Bill for children between the age group of 5 and 14 years. Urgent action is needed for providing suitable school infrastructure and appointment of good teachers for running the schools for providing quality education to the children blended with the modern technologies of e-learning and teleeducation. While doing so a review of the syllabus is also required to prevent overloading of the children for ensuring blossoming of their creativity.

**Protecting the Brand Image of Higher Education:** The nations vision of developed India requires greater thrust to scientific and technological advancements. All our IITs, IIMs have graduated as world class brand institutions in addition to the century old premier institution as, Indian Institute of Science, Bangalore. These characteristics must be preserved and nurtured. We should also encourage universities to become cradles of higher learning and research, contributing generation of high skilled global human resource force.

**Examination Reforms:** Often, we have witnessed that many important national examinations have been the target of attack by a select group of corrupt individuals who undermine the very fabric of secrecy and transparency of the conduct of these examinations. While we should deal with such individuals with sternness to protect the image of our national selection system and the quality, we should also find technological solution that can ensure tamper proof examination system.

## Agriculture and Agrofood Processing

With farmers in focus, farming technology as their friend, and food processing and marketing as partners is indeed the second green revolution. From now on to 2020, India would have to gradually increase the production to around 400 million tones per annum. The increase in the production will have to be done under the reduced availability of land from 170 million hectares to 100 million hectares with reduced water availability using technological inputs.

## Pharmaceuticals

Institutions of Pharmaceutical Sciences and Pharma Industries need to evolve an integrated and comprehensive National Pharma Vision to meet the challenges of design to drug development, production and marketing. The major challenge before the Pharma community is to prevent the entry of spurious drugs and eradicate its presence in the market.

## Space

With our self-reliance in our Space programme it is the time that we should enter into the global market aggressively. The exploration of the moon through 'Chandrayaan' and keeping our sight on the Mars will electrify the entire country, particularly young scientists and children.

## Defence

Modernization of our armed forces with force multipliers is indeed progressing to meet the national security needs. Defence technology has led to the development of long range missile systems and supersonic cruise missile, Light Combat Aircraft, Electronic warfare systems, radars, under-water sensors, combat vehicles and armaments. The Indo-Russian joint venture programme – BRAHMOS is one of the leading examples of development, production and marketing of state-of-the-art missile system.

## Energy

Our power generation capacity of hundred thousand Megawatt has to be tripled by the year 2020. In addition to the power generation from the conventional sources we need to enhance the power generation capacity through non-conventional energy sources to attain power security. Also the present nuclear capacity of 2700 Megawatts should be enhanced to more than 20,000 Megawatts by 2020. Desalination plants can be co-located with the future nuclear power plants for converting sea water to drinking water. We need to establish large solar farms of 800 to 1000 Megawatts capacity in many areas to augment the energy requirements.

## S&T Growth

Every academic institution and R&D Organisation is a reservoir of knowledge. Technology will also spin off to societal products, which are cost-effective, high-quality and available to the people in time. Thrust is required in Nano-science and biotechnology to achieve leadership in these areas in the coming decade. The scientists and technologists must undertake a health mission, "Let my brain remove the pain." The scientific community must realize that the competitiveness can come only by integrated mission driven programmes partnered by academy, R&D organisation and industry.

## Civic Awareness

The status of environmental cleanliness is one of the indicators of development of a nation. As a nation, we have to keep our environment clean and tidy. This is essential for better health conditions of all the citizens and also for presenting a wholesome and aesthetic atmosphere for us and also the tourists visiting our country. It is essential that we keep all our places of worship and rivers clean and tidy to preserve their innate divinity. Each one of the States may promulgate appropriate local laws for promoting harmonious environment in their regions.

## Election Manifesto

The general elections for 14th Lok Sabha will take place in 2004. I was thinking what could be the manifesto of the competing political parties for the election. India has more than 540 million people upto the age of 25 years. India is a nation of youth. During my interactions with the youth of our country, two aspects have come out very clearly. One is that the young have a passion, self-respect and dream to live in developed India. Second, they want to live in a corruption free India. I can see these two are glowing in their eyes. I am also convinced that we should build developed India in a time bound way to prevent instability in the society. Hence the manifesto of the political parties has to take into account their aspirations and design them to meet the dream of the young and be resonant with their aspirations with identified missions and action plan. Every political party must clearly state their vision, action plan, and approaches for the developed India vision 2020 and how fast they can realize these missions in quality and quantity.

## Voter's Responsibility

Every citizen has got a role to choose the right representative to the Parliament and Legislatures, whose vision is that of national development and who has the concern for his/her constituency and the people. The right to vote is the greatest power given by the democracy to you, so that you can reinforce further democratic values. I would like to appeal to all eligible voters to exercise their franchise without fail, fear or favour. Large voter turn out will be the first step towards realization of developed India 2020, and the second step would be to become enlightened righteous citizens.

## 'Movement' by Young Citizens

Which is the starting point, for the character evolution in the nation? Let me share with you an incident, which took place somewhere in Nagaland. I was talking to a group of 600 persons consisting of young children, their parents and teachers. The topic I selected was the knowledge society, foundation for a developed India. One boy who was studying in 10th class, asked me, "Mr. President, tell me is it possible for a nation to get transformed into a developed country, when there is corruption everywhere?" This question greatly upset the many faces of the experienced generation. I said that, "The question was beautiful and I must answer." Fortunately, the boys parents and teachers were sitting by his side. I asked both, "Do you have an answer?" They said, "Mr. President, he shouldn't have asked such a question, which is beyond his age. Please ignore it, Sir." How can I ignore such a valuable mind? I must answer. My answer was the following.

We can create any number of laws in the country. No law can remove corruption fully. However there are only three members of the society, who can remove corruption. I call it as a "Three-dimensional action," plan. Who are these three members? They are father, mother and elementary school teacher. In this connection, I would like to recall a famous statement from Vedic Guru, who said, "You give me a child for seven years after that, no God or devil can change the child." That is the power of the teacher.

When you hear my broadcast to the nation, please ask yourself a question, what can be the greatest contribution that the youth can give without disturbing their academic pursuit. You have to commence a silent revolution for removal of corruption by rightly reforming those who go against righteousness in your families. You all must endeavour to make the home you live, beautiful and righteous. You definitely have the power on your parents to do so, with love and affection.

Now I would like to administer an oath for the youth which I would like the youths to repeat with me now, wherever you are. Are you ready?

## Ten Point Oath for the Youth of the Nation

1. I will pursue my education or the work with dedication and I will excel in it.
2. From now onwards, I will teach at least 10 persons to read and write those who cannot read and write.
3. I will plant at least 10 saplings and shall ensure their growth through constant care.
4. I will visit rural and urban areas and permanently wean away at least 5 persons from addiction and gambling.
5. I will constantly endeavour to remove the pain of my suffering brethren.
6. I will not support any religious, caste or language differentiation.
7. I will be honest and endeavour to make a corruption-free society.
8. I will work for becoming an enlightened citizen and make my family righteous.
9. I will always be a friend of the mentally and

physically challenged and will work hard to make them feel normal, like the rest of us.

10. I will proudly celebrate the success of my country and my people.

## Conclusion

India is very fortunate to have 540 million youth out of a billion people. We are doing well in agriculture, our industry is on the upswing and our performance in the services sector is also equally good. Time has now come for us to make our country, righteous. Righteousness comes out of good character. The evolution of good character leads to harmony in home. Harmony in home brings the people of the state to become enlightened citizens. Enlightened citizens lead the planet earth to be a peaceful world.

□

---

*Address to the Nation on the Eve of 55th Republic Day, New Delhi on 25-01-2004.*

# 23
# Challenge to Science

## Great things – How do we Achieve in Science?

One incident, which happened during a programme for honouring Prof. Norman E Borlaug with Dr. M.S. Swaminathan Award, at Vigyan Bhavan, New Delhi on the 15th of March 2005. Prof. Norman E. Borlaug, at the age of 91 was in the midst of all the praise showered on him from everybody. First, he talked about India's advancement in the agricultural science and agricultural production and the present status of agricultural science in India. He turned to the dais; he talked about Dr. M.S. Swaminathan and a political visionary late Shri C. Subramaniam who were the prime architects of First Green Revolution in India. He also recalled about Dr. V. Kurien who was the father of White Revolution in India. Then he turned to the audience and started identifying scientists such as Dr. Raja Ram, a wheat specialist, Dr. S.K. Vasal, a maize specialist, Dr. B.R. Barwale, a seed specialist who was contributing in the agricultural advancement in India and abroad. Dr. Borlaug introduced them to the audience by asking them to stand and ensured that the audience cheered and greeted them with great enthusiasm. Here, I noticed a unique way of a 91 year old Nobel Laureate, who remembered and recognised all the key contributors to the agriculture mission irrespective of their position. This lesson, I would like the Indian scientific community to observe and follow, while dealing with all young scientists.

In another incident, my friend Dr. Vasant Gowariker sent me an executive summary of The Fertilizer Encyclopedia prepared by him and his team. The comment by Dr. Norman E. Borlaug on this document is noteworthy. I quote: Asian farmers in particular must now judiciously increase their per hectare use of fertilizer, looking for greater efficiency in use and also in dealing with deficiencies of secondary and minor elements of the soil? Unquote. This is how he sets the targets and provides encouragement for pursuing science across the world.

Another unique personality whom I remember, when I talk about science is Prof. C.N.R. Rao. I have visited his laboratory. He is a pioneer and an example of leading from the front. His research started from structure of molecules and that opened newer frontiers in surface sciences and more recently in nanoparticles and nanomaterials. He is one of the highly decorated Indian scientists. He is a motivator par excellence and pursues science with passion. Among the many awards he has received for his contribution in science, I would like to particularly mention the prestigious 'Dan David Prize' given to him by Dan David Prize Foundation headquartered at Tel Aviv University for his contribution towards the future time dimension in the filed of material science. In addition, he is the first recipient of 'India Science Award' announced on 28 February, 2005.

Another important scientist in the field of medicine, I would like to recall is Dr. P. Venugopal, Director, All India Institute of Medical Sciences, New Delhi. In his laboratory, he pioneered stem cell research in the field of cardiology. One of the cardiac diseases, where conventional medical and surgical treatment were ineffective because of the affliction of the heart muscle, stem cells implantation into the diseased heart muscles had been applied in order to improve the function of heart muscle. This kind of application of this procedure is the latest and very few cases have been done in the world, the first time in India. This is expected to open new frontiers in the treatment of patients for regeneration of heart muscles, thereby giving new hope for the patients suffering end stage heart disease. The commitment of Dr. P. Venugopal for research ultimately results in saving hundreds of lives.

I have mentioned these names only to assure ourselves that the Indian science has great future.

## Empowering the Young Scientists

I remember an incident with Prof. Vikram Sarabhai during the 1960s. There were a few scientists and technologists, whom Dr. Sarabhai nurtured. I would like to share with you how he nurtured them. Whenever he comes to Trivandrum, I used to discuss with him the proposal for the development of Composite Products. At that time I was in the initial stages of my career as rocket engineer, with less than 2 years of experience in ISRO.

Similarly, there was Dr. S.C. Gupta, a specialist in guidance and Dr. Amba Rao a specialist in Aerospace structures. In spite of our being just introduced into the organisation with few years of experience, noticing our interest in development of certain materials and systems Dr. Sarabhai funded for the creation of laboratories. He created fibre composite laboratory based on my proposal, which later became Reinforced Plastic Centre. He created Gyro laboratory centered on the expertise of Dr. Gupta, which later became Guidance Laboratory and space structures laboratory centered around Dr. Amba Rao, which later become advanced dynamics group. These centres became the centres of excellence and incubated many advanced technology missions that fed critical inputs to space programme. Once the potential of the young scientist is understood, the heads of the organisation must invest on them boldly irrespective of the positions of the scientists and their age considerations. If this philosophy is pursued with sincerity the research would flourish and youth would be encouraged to embrace science.

**Great Indian Scientists**

In India, science and technology took a two-phase progress with the momentum created in 1930s, by the great scientists of international repute. They gave the country the confidence. We may remember the pioneering contributions to science made by Chandrasekhar Subramaniam for his Chandrasekhar limit and black hole, Sir C.V. Raman for his discovery of the 'Raman Effect', Srinivasa Ramanujan for his contributions towards number theory, J.C. Bose in the area of microwaves, Meghnad Saha for, 'Thermo-Ionization Equation'. This phase, I consider the glorious phase of Indian science. This scientific foundation laid by them always triggered the later generations also. The unique similarities of all these scientists are the one that they had dedicated their entire life for the cause of scientific research and the spirit of inquiry for the fields that they have chosen amidst all the hurdles and problems in their life as well as their career. Science always gives life time missions to the scientists, and then only success comes. They have not deviated towards the other worldly prospects or towards their own career advancements. This quality helped them to make singular contributions for the benefit of science and the world. It is a question of dedication, commitment and understanding and also the environment for research in science, which gives birth to the scientists for the nation. They inspired many later generation scientists including G.N. Ramachandran, the originator of triple-helix.

Let me now discuss on how India has attracted large number of scientists and engineers towards drawing the roadmap for achieving self-reliance in critical technologies in defence, space and atomic energy.

**The Post-independence Phase of Indian Science and Technology**

All of us know, in history, any country reposes its confidence initially among a few stout and earnest knowledge giants. Particularly I took interest to study the lives of three scientists, as I was interested in their scientific technological leadership qualities that focused the relationship of S&T and development of the nation. In the history of India, there may be many but I was very close to these three great personalities for one reason or the other. They are founders of three great institutions. I worked in two of the institutions directly and one in partnership. Dr. D.S. Kothari, a Professor in Delhi University was an outstanding Physicist with special interest in Astrophysics. He is well-known for ionization of matter by pressure in cold compact objects like planets. This theory is complementary to epoch making theory of thermal ionization of his Guru Dr. Meghnad Saha. Dr. D.S. Kothari set a scientific tradition in Indian defence tasks when he became Scientific Adviser to Defence Minister in 1948. The first thing he did was to establish the Defence Science Centre to do research in electronic material, nuclear medicine and ballistic science. He is considered as the architect of defence science in India. His race continued and followed up with a momentum working and contributing in the areas of strategic systems, electronic warfare systems, armaments and life sciences.

Now, let me discuss about Homi Jehangir Bhabha. He did research in theoretical physics in Cambridge University. During 1930-1939, Homi Bhabha carried out research relating to cosmic radiation. In 1939, he joined Sir C.V. Raman in IISc Bangalore. Later, he was asked to start Tata Institute of Fundamental Research with focus on nuclear science and mathematical science. He subsequently established Indian Atomic Energy Commission in 1948. Multicenters were born with his vision in nuclear science to nuclear technology, nuclear power, nuclear devices and nuclear medicine. These science institutions established multitechnological centers, but basic science was the vital component.

The youngest of the three was Prof. Vikram Sarabhai and he worked with Sir C.V. Raman in experimental cosmic ray. Prof. Sarabhai established Physical Research Laboratory in Ahmedabad with Space Research as focus. In later years he became the Director of Space S&T Centre. The SSTC (1963) started with the launching of sounding rockets for space atmospheric research. His vision transformed Indian Space Research Organisation (ISRO) into multiple space technology centers. These centers are responsible for development and leading to launch of PSLV in the sun synchronous orbit. And we have also witnessed a launching of GSLV in the geosynchronous orbit with communication satellite.

Three personalities, Dr. D.S. Kothari, Dr. Homi Bhabha and Dr. Vikram Sarabhai were physicists, who went on to build huge S&T institutions that became the home of more than 20,000 young scientists and engineers and also the kindler of their innovativeness. I believe strongly that if the three scientists had gone on to concentrate only on science, at least one of them would have got the Nobel Prize, but India would not have had the advantage of having the atomic energy, space and defence research establishments in the country with this magnitude. We must take the message and the mission of successful scientists such as Raman, Chandrasekhar, Kothari, Homi Bhabha and Sarabhai to the youth so that they will understand the various ways by which one could contribute to the growth of the nation, if they take science as a career. This would surely attract many young people towards science.

## Importance of Science in the Present Context

As soon as we became independent, the country was infested with problems to bring in urgently needed technologies for steel, civil structures, hydro dams and thermal power stations. Our concentration was directed towards solving burning problems like feeding the population, providing water, shelter and health care. The political visionaries at that time, in spite of our having a very weak economy, decided to wisely set up what ultimately has become the science base of our country such as Atomic Energy, Space, CSIR, DRDO, DST etc. The country also set up the powerful educational base including the creation of IITs and many universities, which had a unique blend of science and technology.

Today the country has become one of the strongest in the world in terms of scientific manpower in capability and maturity. Our economy has also become strong. Hence, we are in a position not only to understand the technologies that we may have to borrow, but also to create our own technologies with extensive scientific inputs of indigenous origin. This, in fact, would do a value addition. In many areas such as Pharma, we are delivering to the world, products which are backed by large amount of R&D. Basically we have come a long way since our independence, from mere buyers of technology to those of who have made science and technology as an important contributor for national development and societal transformation. In a world where the powers are determined by their share of the worlds knowledge, reflected by patents, papers and so on, the WTO starts to play a crucial role in the economic development. It is important for India to put all her acts together to become a continuous innovator and creator of science and technology intensive products. The science that we do today must have the innovativeness and the foresight and the vision for it to be the centre of the technology that we develop tomorrow for the competitive world.

## Scientific Challenges for the Future

In the last three decades, we have witnessed an

unstinted growth in miniaturization of IT products in the world. Central to this is the silicon technology. The feature size of the transistors has been decreasing relentlessly. It is predicted that the miniaturization using silicon microelectronics will find its plateau and its limit will be reached within the next decade. The world is on the lookout for an alternative to silicon. The transformation from microelectronics to the nanoscience and nanotechnology is knocking at our doors. The endless alternatives include molecular transistors, quantum computing, nanoelectronics and so on. India has the good science base needed for being a pioneer in making this breakthrough a reality.

In addition to the above, the challenges facing Indian scientists in the coming decades will be the development of anti vaccine for HIV/AIDS and development of seeds for agricultural products which requires minimum water and can provide high yield per hectare to compensate the reduced availability of land. Apart from this, there is a need to work on thorium based nuclear power plants, integrated mission for stem cell research, launching of hypersonic reusable launch vehicle and take discoveries and innovations to provide better quality of life to the differently challenged people. These are some of the challenges facing the scientific community in the coming decades.

**Conclusion**

I would like to make the following suggestions for attracting the young people to careers in Science.

1. It is essential to have an assured career in science for a certain number of high quality committed scientists with aptitude towards research. There should be a minimum annual intake of about 300 M.Sc. and 100 Ph.D scientists with proper emoluments and assured career growth in the organisations such as ISRO, DRDO, Atomic Energy, CSIR, DST and the Universities. The private and government funded

universities must be encouraged to appoint M.Sc and Ph.D. who have been selected through a nationally coordinated competitive selection process. This will be a great motivator for the science students and also their parents for pursuing advanced courses in science. This is the first and foremost need for attracting young people to career in science, an assurance to the youth and the parents that the future is secure, once they take science as a career.

2. The experienced scientists and policy-makers of the organisations must recognize the talents available in the organisation irrespective of the position and empower the young scientists to create state-of-the-art laboratories once they have concrete thoughts and vision. Prof. Vikram Sarabhai in the initial stages of ISRO brought in a culture of management which encouraged and satisfied the vision of the young scientists which collectively succeeded in making the mission of the organisation a reality.
3. Universities and Research and Development institutions must encourage and facilitate the young scientists to write quality research papers in frontier areas and in prestigious journals. They should also facilitate the youth to present the papers in national and international seminars and symposiums which will enable them to assess their standard against international benchmarks. Encouraging youth to be lead authors while publishing the joint research would be a very good gesture that the youngsters would cherish for many years.
4. Based on my experience during my interaction with the 600,000 students, I realize that they are looking for role models, whom they would like to follow after their 10+2 career. Approximately 7 million students appear for plus two examinations every

year. Out of which 3 million students are from the science stream. To attract this youth towards a career in science, we need many novel ideas. The youth must be made to understand the beauty of doing science, the pleasure of doing science and the ultimate bliss when the results of science make you understand the nature, master it, control it and finally make things that improve the quality of life of the human kind. Every one of us, scientists must pledge that we will at least spend sometime visiting the schools to ignite the young minds by recounting our own experiences.

□

*Address at the Inauguration of the Seminar on 'Attracting Young People to Careers in Science', Indian Physics Association IIT, New Delhi on 31-03-2005.*

# 24

# Electro Magnet Spectrum: A Friend of the Humanity

The domain of URSI extends throughout the solar system and out among the galaxies. I am sure that when man reaches the outermost limit of the observable universe he will be assisted by means of radio for communicating with earth from the space platform for navigation and control using electromagnetic waves envisaged by Maxwell, J.C. Bose and Marconi about a century ago. International Union of Radio Science (URSI) offers an excellent opportunity to the radio scientists particularly young scientists to interact with international experts on state-of-the-art subjects.

## Study of Upper Atmospheric Electrojet

I am reminded of an event which took place on November 21, 1963, when I was a rocket engineer at Thumba. This was a very important day in the history of India's space programme. On that day, the first sounding rocket from India was launched from Thumba with international cooperation. The rocket and payload was integrated in the Thumba Equatorial Rocket Launching Station (TERLS). The rocket carried the sodium vapour payload to study the upper atmospheric winds and Longmuir wave probe to study the upper atmospheric electrojet. This first experiment, paved the way for many sounding rocket experiments and TERLS was dedicated, to the international scientific community, for the unique experiments in the electro magnetic jet, as India was uniquely placed near electro magnetic equator to study electrojet and related phenomena in the ionosphere. The 1963 rocket launch from Thumba was my first experience with radio propagation and related studies. The starting of Thumba Equatorial Rocket Launching Station (TERLS) was the seeding of India's space programme. Since Prof. Vikram Sarabhai was the founder for the Physical Research Laboratory at Ahmedabad which was spearheading the space research, TERLS became the laboratory for space experiments.

Here I would like to mention the contribution of Prof. Vikram Sarabhai who worked on experimental cosmic ray, Dr. Homi Jegangir Bhabha who carried out research relating to cosmic radiation and Dr. Kothari who is well-known for his work on ionization on matter by pressure in cold compact objects like planets. Apart from their contribution in their areas of specialization, Prof. Vikram Sarabhai sowed the seeds for ISRO, Dr. Homi Jegangir Bhabha, architect of nuclear science, created the Department of Atomic Energy and Dr. Kothari was the architect of defence science in India. We are proud of the contribution made by these three physicists in building three great scientific and technological institutions to nurture and grow science and technology in our country. Today the space programme through its sounding rocket programme and geosynchronous satellite programme is contributing for India's communication covering the major electromagnetic spectrum.

**Radio Communication: Life Line of Projects**

In the early days of space programme, for overseas communications, we used to have wireless communication link between Trivandrum and Mumbai for onward connectivity to the rest of the country and outside world. Similarly, in the early phase of missile programme, the communication link between Hyderabad and Chandipur, Balasore was also through wireless sets. In fact, the entire operational communication systems between Wheeler Island, Main Land, Balasore, SHAR, Down Range Ships and Car Nicobar were through HF wireless communication links. These communication facilities made me understand the value of robust noise free radio communications and the role of scientists and engineers in realizing these systems for real application.

**Child's Fantasy**

Recently, I found the visualization of a 13 year old girl named Aardhra Krishna on how the earth's civilization will look like around 3000 AD. In her imagination, the citizens are forced to migrate to Mars and have made Mars the home to a flourishing civilization. This advanced civilization, which was man-made, comes suddenly under threat created by nature in the form of an asteroid of Jupiter. The asteroid from Jupiter orbit was coming towards Mars and Mars was in danger of extinction. The scientists on Mars come up with a very innovative plan of a barrage of nuclear cannons to attack the oncoming asteroid. The bombardment destroys the asteroid and the year 3000 sees a Martian civilization surviving from the fury of the nature by an innovative scientific application. What a wonderful scientific and technological thinking of the young mind? Will it all be possible without the availability of Radio Science which transmits large amount of information encompassing the entire solar system? When I was admiring this imagination of the young student, a real time space experiment took place that gave some meaning to the imagination of the youth.

**Combating Asteroids**

On 4th July 2005 one important event took place in space. That was the impact of the NASA spacecraft called deep impact smashing into the comet Tempel-I, with enough force to create football stadium sized crater with a depth of a 14 storey-building. The spacecraft was navigated through a ground control system by an Indian, Shyam Bhaskaran – the deep impact travelled 431 million kms in 172 days escaping from the earth orbit and intercepted the comet at a straight distance from earth at 134 million km. The comet was orbiting around the Sun every five and half years. This is a landmark in radio communications and space exploration.

This event is an important milestone to develop standardised technique for combating asteroids which may hit the earth in future. One such large asteroid (1950 AD) is predicted with certain probability to hit the earth on March 16, 2880 AD and nearly one third of the earth would be damaged. Like the 'Deep Impact', many spacecraft will be required to be sent with high energy material particles to divert or break the asteroid to move it out of the dangerous orbit. All this is possible only if we have a reliable robust radio communication system.

## Binary Millisecond Pulsar

One of the important areas of application of radio science in India is the discovery of binary millisecond pulsar. A pulsar is the remnant of a star which exploded, leaving behind a sphere made up of neutrons just 20 km in size but weighing more than the sun. The pulsar emits a beam of radio wave which is seen from the earth as a pulse every time it rotates. These waves are very weak, when they reach the earth. In order to detect the pulsar, one needs facilities like the Giant Meter Wave Radio Telescope (GMRT). The Tata Institute of Fundamental Research (TIFR) has built this largest Radio telescope in the world in rural area near the village of Khodad, 80 km from Pune. Because of the unique capabilities of our GMRT, scientists from all over the world, including USA and Canada, visit the centre to conduct collaborative experiments. Our scientists played a leading role in the recent discovery of a new, "Binary millisecond pulsar." Discoveries like the one that has been made by the scientists of the National Centre for Radio Astrophysics of TIFR, is an important contribution for our radio science. Particularly I greet the team lead by Prof. Govind Swarup.

## Earthquake Forecast and Electromagnetic Phenomena

In many places in our planet, we experience severe earthquakes resulting in loss of life, loss of wealth and in some cases it destroys the decades of progress made by the country and its valuable civilizational heritage. India has earthquake problems periodically in certain regions. Recently, in our state of Jammu and Kashmir and the neighbouring country, there was an earthquake. US, Japan, Turkey, Iran and many other countries also suffer due to earthquakes.

Earthquake is a subterrain phenomenon and predicting this from space observations would be a great challenge. An Earthquake phenomenon in broader sense starts to produce some precursors before the final rupture, although this precursor generating pre-rupture stage is not usually regarded as part of an earthquake. The question is whether such precursor really exists or not. So-called pre-slip envisaged in the dynamic models of earthquake source is also a good theoretical possibility but its observation appears difficult. Precise geodetic measurement by GPS may succeed in the detection of the pre-slip. It seems that electromagnetic phenomena prior to final rupture may be promising. According to new concepts earthquakes occur when the crust reaches a critical state, emission of electromagnetic signals before final rupture is theoretically plausible, notably in the ultra low frequency (ULF) range and very low frequency (VLF) range.

It is hoped that well organised electromagnetic monitoring may provide unique observational information on the pre-slips. Atmospheric/ionospheric anomalies still remains unresolved. Post-earthquake disaster recovery, communication and damage assessment are also areas where space science and communication technology can quickly make its impact. I am sure radio scientists will definitely be keen to establish the correlation between the occurrence of earthquake and the electromagnetic disturbances noticed in the specific region.

**Disaster Warning System**

It is important to mention and acknowledge the contributions made by the Amateur radio operators called HAMs, who started using radio communication technique particularly the shortwave for long distance communication through the ionosphere during the first decade of 20th century. The experience of HAMs has been used for remote area, disaster management and emergency communication world-over during the last hundred years. NASA, ISRO and other space agencies have honoured the HAMs by launching exclusive satellite for them so that they can continue to contribute in the latest trends of satellite communication. During the recent Tsunami it was a coincidence that a Government of India approved amateur radio expedition was in Andaman and was operational during the disaster and provided vital communications to the main land and Indonesia for getting latest updates on the movement of Tsunami waves and rescue operations. The contributions made by Indian HAMs in this Tsunami have been acknowledged at national and international level. Amateur radio and remote area communication are synonymous with emergency communication. It is advisable to promote this hobby to set up amateur radio stations in Panchayats offices, schools and hospitals by voluntary agencies who will be able to locate and operate the HAMs throughout the day and night, on all days. Each Panchayat must encourage this hobby and can make it as a part of the village knowledge centre. This will act as an early warning system for the village community in case of an unforeseen eventuality. At this hour, I would like to remember fondly the significant contribution of the Late Dr. Shrikant Jichkar in promoting HAMs in India.

Commercial radio communication system operates with high power, frequency diversity with large antenna to improve the reliability of communication. HAMs work with limited power under man-made and natural radio interference and work in difficult circumstances. There is a lot of scope to improve narrowband communication technique multihop HF communication to remote areas such as Antarctica and Arctic to improve the quality of HAM communication. The members of the radio science community can definitely assist the HAM operators through research in establishing low cost narrowband communication techniques.

**Space Industrial Revolution**

India is in the mission of transforming into a developed country. Many developed countries are racing towards Moon and Mars which may lead to the next industrial revolution. We also have the opportunity of joining this exclusive club of nations to establish industry in Moon and Mars with our core competence in space science and technology. The technological challenges are:

- Manufacturing and Mining in reduced gravity.
- Harnessing Helium-3 in Moon for future energy, using oncoming fusion technologies.
- Using dry ice deposits in Moon and Mars as source of fuel rocket engine.
- Extending life of satellites in orbit through refuelling and repairing.
- Using the Moon as space transportation hub.
- Building human habitats on the Moon, Mars and also in outer space.

- Above all, it is essential to establish reliable space communication systems that will work during all ionospheric disturbance and sunspot activities.

## Lunar Telecommunications Base

Characteristics of moon have a vital implication for space science. As civilization spreads to Mars in five to eight decades, the Moon will provide the main link between earth and her scattered children. The earth's ionosphere reflects all but the shortest radio waves back to Earth. Earth's dynamic atmosphere prevents the use of lasers for communication into space. On the near airless Moon, this would not be a problem, for the Moon's sky is perennially clear to waves of all frequencies. Thus the Moon will soon become a 'Telecommunications Hub', for interplanetary communications, aiming its tightly focused laser beams to other planets and ships in space. With interplanetary communication systems located on the far side, the Moon would also shield these communication stations from the continuous radio emissions from the earth. The far side of the Moon would be the quietest place within millions of kilometers from the earth, in the sense of radio silence. The coming few decades will provide a great challenge to the radio scientists.

## Conclusion

I would like to make the following seven suggestions to scientific community which will be useful to the entire mankind.

(1) There has been a revolution in communication science and technology all over the world. The result of this revolution has to reach the common man. This can be in the form of providing affordable high bandwidth telecommunication to every villager, such as mobile phones with GPRS/CDMA, satellite and FM radio and IP communication. Research

is required to bring down the cost and make this revolution reach seamlessly to six billion people of the world.

(2) The power of radio communication needs to be utilised for improving the educational standards of our rural masses. Recently, I was addressing the students of three universities in three different regions of the country from Rashtrapati Bhavan. While organizing this event I found that the connectivity to various corners in the country is yet to become seamless. The radio and space communication specialists have to work together to make high bandwidth seamless connectivity for the teleeducation programmes to reach our distant villages with ease through broadband communication.

(3) There are possibilities of correlation between the seismic activities, electromagnetic activity in the particular region. There is a need to have a comprehensive study on the subject. This study should also be linked with the study of other geophysical parameters relevant to an earthquake. This will be a great contribution of the radio science community to the mankind towards disaster mitigation.

(4) India is in the process of establishing three Science centres in different parts of the country to create a scientific research cadre. The URSI can evolve a possible curriculum for study and research in the electro magnetic spectrum in these advanced centres.

(5) I understand that the adaptive radio and software radio are among the thrust areas of wireless communication technologies. In this connection, it is essential for the radio scientists to provide a solution for getting high bandwidth communication

in the wireless spectrum in a mobile environment for an optimal distance without the constraints of line of sight.

(6) Radio scientists and technologists should continue to strive for optimum and bandwidth efficient communication techniques even when higher frequency bands like millimeter waves, sub-millimeter waves and quasioptical waves have started becoming available; there is not much congestion at this stage in this frequency band, but the ever increasing use of radio frequencies spectrum needs evolution of an allocation criteria.

(7) Solar power satellites may become a reality in few decades. Because of its potential for transmitting large volume of power in Gigawatts, the possible electric power transmission is through microwave to the earth. Research is essential to find out the relationship of transmitting frequency with atmospheric structure.

I find that radio science embraces all areas of human activity such as provision of cost-effective communication to all the citizens, education, healthcare, development, disaster mitigation, earthquake forecasting and solution to energy problem. In overall perspective, connectivity is the key for the growth of the humanity. Hence, radio scientists have a major role to play with their continuing research in promoting economic prosperity to the planet Earth through uninterrupted connectivity.

□

---

*Address at the Inauguration of General Assembly of International Union of Radio Sciences (URSI), New Delhi on 22-10-2005.*

# 25

# Enriching the Society through Education

Any University is judged by the level and extent of the research work it accomplishes. This sets in a regenerative cycle of excellence. Experience of research leads to quality teaching and quality teaching imparted to the young in turn enriches the research. Research brings transformation and development and also enhances the quality of education. Both the research and teaching are being carried out in the best traditions of Mizoram University. Let me share with this important gathering on the two phase progress of science and technology in India.

## Scientific Scene in Pre-independent India

In India, science and technology took a two-phase progress with the momentum created in 1930s, by the great scientists of international repute. They gave the country the confidence. We remember the pioneering contributions to science made by Chandrasekhar Subramaniam for his Chandrasekhar limit and black hole, Sir C.V. Raman for his discovery of the "Raman effect", Srinivasa Ramanujan for his contributions towards number theory, JC Bose in the area of microwaves, S.N. Bose, famous for Bose-Einstein statistics and Meghnad Saha for "Thermo-Ionization Equation." This phase, I consider the glorious phase of Indian science. The scientific foundation laid by them triggered the later generations. The unique similarities of all these scientists are the one that they had dedicated their entire life for the cause of scientific research and the spirit of inquiry for the fields that they have chosen amidst all the hurdles and problems in their life. Science always gives life time missions to the scientists, and then only success comes. It is a question of dedication, commitment and understanding and also the environment for research in science, which gives birth to the scientists for the nation. They inspired many later generation scientists including GN Ramachandran, the originator of triple-helix.

Let me now discuss on how India had built the S&T base and drew the road map leading to national development using science and technologies particularly in the field of defence, space and atomic energy in the post independent era. The science and technology had also fed critical inputs to reaching self-sufficiency in food through the Green Revolution and milk production through the White Revolution.

## The Post-independence Phase of Indian Science and Technology

All of you know, in history, any country revolves itself initially around a few stout and earnest knowledge giants. Particularly I took interest to study the lives of three scientists, as I was interested in their scientific technological leadership qualities that focused the relationship of S&T and development of the nation. In the history of India, there may be many but I was very close to these three great personalities for one reason or the other. They are founders of three great institutions. I worked in two of the institutions directly and one in partnership. Dr. D.S. Kothari, a Professor in Delhi University was an outstanding Physicist and also an Astrophysicist. He is well-known for ionization of matter by pressure in cold compact objects like planets. This theory is complementary to thermal ionization work done by Dr. Meghnad Saha his Guru. Dr. D.S. Kothari set a scientific tradition in Indian defence tasks when he became Scientific Adviser to Defence Minister in 1948; He created a Board of Advisors to the Scientific Advisor consisting of Dr. H.J. Bhabha, Dr. K.S. Krishnan and Dr. S.S. Bhatnagar. Later the Board was renamed as Scientific Advisory Board with enlarged membership.

He established the Defence Science Centre to do research in electronic material, nuclear medicine and ballistic science. He is considered as the architect of defence science in India. His race continued and followed up with momentum working and contributing in the areas of strategic systems, electronic warfare systems, armaments and life sciences.

## Pioneer in Indian Nuclear Science

Homi Jehangir Bhabha did research in theoretical physics in Cambridge University. During 1930-1939, Homi Bhabha carried out research relating to cosmic radiation. In 1939, he joined Sir C.V. Raman in IISc Bangalore. Later, he was asked to start the Tata Institute of Fundamental Research (TIFR) with focus on nuclear science, mathematical science and established Atomic Energy Commission in 1948. Multicenters were born with his vision in nuclear science to nuclear technology, nuclear power, nuclear devices and nuclear medicine. These science institutions established multitechnological centers with basic science as a vital component. I am sure our nuclear scientists and technologists will add to our country 20,000 MW power by the year 2020 as the vision propounded by our Department of Atomic Energy.

## Indian Space Visionary

Prof. Vikram Sarabhai, the youngest of the three, worked with Sir C.V. Raman in experimental cosmic ray research. Prof. Sarabhai established Physical Research

Laboratory (PRL) Ahmedabad with space research as focus. PRL was the cradle of Indian Space Programme. Prof. Vikram Sarabhai unfurled the space mission for India in 1970 that we should build Satellite Launch Vehicle capability, to put our communication satellites in the geosynchronous orbit and remote sensing satellites in the polar orbit. Also, he envisaged that launch vehicles built in India should be launched from Indian soil. This one visionary thought led to intensive research and development in multiple fields of science and space technology. Many of us had the fortune to be part of Prof. Vikram Sarabhai's vision. My team and myself participated in India's first satellite launch vehicle programme to put the satellite in the orbit. Today, India with her 20,000 scientific, technological and support staff in multiple space research centres, supported by about 300 industries and academic institutions, has the capability to build any type of satellite launch vehicle to place remote sensing, communication and meteorology satellites in different orbits and space application has become part of our daily life. Dear young friends, you have seen how visionaries of a nation, bring about economic transformation and technological change. I would like you to emulate these visionaries, dream and work for transforming India into a developed nation.

## Nurturing the Talent

Prof. Borlaug, a Nobel Laureate and a well-known agricultural scientist, at the age of 91 was in the midst of all the praise showered on him from everybody gathered there. When his turn came, he got up and highlighted India's advancement in the agricultural science and production and said that the political visionary Shri C. Subramaniam and Dr. M.S. Swaminathan were the prime architects of First Green Revolution in India. He also recalled with pride, Dr. Verghese Kurien who ushered White Revolution in India. Then the surprise came. He turned to scientists sitting in the third row, fifth row and eighth row of the audience. He identified Dr. Raja Ram, a wheat specialist, Dr. S.K. Vasal, a maize specialist, Dr. B.R. Barwale, a seed specialist. He said, all these scientists had contributed for your green revolution. Dr. Borlaug introduced them to the audience by asking them to stand and ensured that the audience cheered and greeted the scientists with great enthusiasm. This scene I have not witnessed in our country, so far. This action of Dr. Norman Borlaug, I call it as a Scientific Magnanimity. Young friends, if you aspire to achieve great things in life, you need Scientific Magnanimity. Think about it and correspond with me. It is my experience that great mind and great heart go together. This will motivate the scientific community and nurture team spirit. Here I am reminded of Thiruvalluvars famous Thirukkural:

It means 'The right thoughts become the seeds for the great achievements'.

## Networking of Universities

I would suggest that a website can be created for Universities. This can become a common platform for providing connectivity among the Faculty and students with other universities located in different parts of the country. The website can document the case studies and special achievements of the University and its members and assist new entrants for acquainting themselves with the university. You could also include provision for the students to ask questions about their specific problems connected with education, further studies, research and creation of an enterprise in different places in country.

## Bose-Einstein Dreams

A new form of matter proposed 80 years ago by Indian physicist S N Bose and Albert Einstein has been trapped inside a minute storage ring by scientists at the California University who says the 'blob', might hold key to new quantum physics. The scientists have created a 'blob', of super cooled Bose-Einstein condensate and have kept it running in circles inside a race track two millimeters across. Now you can realize the value of work done by scientists 80 years ago and how it is useful to future scientists. This is the power of science.

## Conclusion

Every one of us has gone through the various phases of education from childhood to profession. A scene appears in front of me. When the child is empowered by the parents, at various phases of growth, the child transforms into a responsible citizen. When the teacher is empowered with knowledge and experience, good young human beings with value systems take shape. When individual or a team is empowered with technology, transformation to higher potential for achievement is assured. When the leader of any institution empowers his or her people, leaders are born who can change the nation in multiple areas. When the women are empowered, society with stability gets assured. When the political leaders of the nation empower the people through visionary policies, the prosperity of the nation is certain.

□□□

---

*Interaction with the Students and Faculty of Mizoram University, Mizoram on 24-09-2005.*